BEHAVIOUR AND PERCEPTION IN
STRANGE ENVIRONMENTS

HELEN E. ROSS

Behaviour and Perception in Strange Environments

BASIC BOOKS, INC., PUBLISHERS
NEW YORK

Printed in Great Britain

Come on, sir; here's the place: – stand still – How fearful
And dizzy 'tis to cast one's eyes so low!
The crows and choughs that wing the midway air
Show scarce so gross as beetles: half way down
Hangs one that gathers samphire, – dreadful trade!
Methinks he seems no bigger than his head:
The fishermen, that walk upon the beach,
Appear like mice; and yond tall anchoring bark,
Diminish'd to her cock, – her cock, a buoy
Almost too small for sight: the murmering surge,
That on the unnumber'd idle pebbles chafes,
Cannot be heard so high. – I'll look no more;
Lest my brain turn, and the deficient sight
Topple down headlong.

Edgar speaking to Gloucester in Shakespeare's *King Lear*,
Act IV, Scene IV

PREFACE

This book has been written as a contribution to the natural history of man's perception and performance in unusual environments. What constitutes an unusual environment has been left fairly vague, as the strangeness varies with the previous experience of the individual: the sea, for example, may be strange to a landlubber, but normal to a sailor. The examples discussed in this book have been selected mainly from environments which the ordinary reader may sometimes experience – such as mountainous country, the underwater world, and fast methods of transport – rather than extreme situations, such as space travel, in which few men can expect to participate. There is already a large amount of psychological literature on the latter topic, but rather less about the more down-to-earth environments. One strange environment which has been extensively studied is the psychological laboratory: we know a great deal about the perception of a one-eyed man with his head in a clamp watching glowing lights in a dark room, but surprisingly little about his perceptual abilities in a real-life situation. This book aims to redress the balance.

The evidence mentioned in this book is catholic: it includes the incidental observations of explorers and travellers, as well as the results of conventional experiments. The references cited are only the tip of an iceberg, but in some areas the submerged mass is deeper than others: in well-worked areas I have generally referred to books or review papers, but in controversial or obscure areas I have tried to give more detail.

I should never have written this book if I had not been introduced to some strange environments by my friends, given much help with the organisation of expeditions and experiments, and benefited from many discussions and new ideas. I should particularly like to thank Alan Baddeley, Bill Hemmings, John Lythgoe and John Woods in connection with diving; Robin Campbell in connection with mountaineering; Richard Gregory for introducing me to the study of perception; and to my husband, John Evans, for reading the manuscript, and inventing new illusions on every outing.

ACKNOWLEDGEMENTS

For permission to use copyright material, acknowledgement is made to the following: Underwater Association (Plate 1); Amer. J. Physics (Fig. 3.4); Dover Publications (Fig. 3.5); Doubleday & Company (Fig. 4.3); Aerospace Medical Association (Plate 6); Harvard University Press (Fig. 5.3); Allen & Unwin (Fig. 7.2).

CONTENTS

ILLUSTRATIONS

CHAPTER 1

Environmental Research

I *The Aims of Research*

It is often maintained that scientific research is, or ought to be, concerned with the testing of theories.[1] The scientist invents a theory, tests it under strictly controlled conditions, and then confirms or revises it in the light of the evidence. This type of research carries high status – particularly if a new theory appears to be confirmed – while data-collecting and naturalistic observations are frowned upon as 'botanising'. Since the prime aim of most academic scientists is to impress other scientists, the majority of research reports are written to fit a theory-confirming paradigm. This distorts the true nature of research, making it appear more logical than it actually is. In fact the researcher often has several ill-defined hypotheses, which he is unable to clarify until the results of the experiments are known; however, he then writes the report as though he could have predicted the results from the start. This practice makes it difficult for the reader to distinguish between genuine theory-testing research, and 'demonstrational research' – the collection and publication of data which apparently confirm a theory.[2] It also discourages researchers from attempting to publish negative findings, or atheoretical work.

On the other hand, many industrial organisations and grant-giving bodies are not interested in the finer points of theory: they prefer research which has practical applications. Grants are very useful tools in furthering a scientific career: they are tokens of success in their own right, and they also enable the scientist to gain additional acclaim from his future research output. The successful researcher learns how to stress the practical value of his work when applying for grants, and its theoretical value when writing it up for scientific journals.

Psychologists seem to suffer from chronic doubt about the type of research that they ought to undertake.[3] This may be because the subject lacks the clearly established norms of the physical sciences. It embraces an almost limitless range of topics and methods, and the choice is bewildering. The safest line of approach for an aspiring psychologist is to stick within a well-established research group, and to work on some self-perpetuating project that earns grants and produces publications. That is the surest way of securing his own advancement.

The proper aim of research should (morally speaking) be the advancement of knowledge rather than the advancement of individuals. Knowledge advances by a variety of methods — hunches, chance observations, systematic data collection, and the revision of theories after controlled experiments. No one method can ensure progress. The researcher who works within a narrow theoretical framework, or in a well-established problem area, is unlikely to make an important new contribution; breakthroughs are more likely to be achieved when someone opens up a new area.[4] Too much attention to one theory makes the scientist consider only the type of data which fits his theory, or which can be studied systematically in his laboratory. Good ideas often arise from the chance association of people, places and problems; but such associations will not occur unless one is open-minded, willing to travel and meet people, and to risk spending time on problems and methods that may not pay off.[5]

II *The Aims and Achievements of Expeditions*

A scientific expedition is a special sort of non-laboratory enterprise. Typically, the participants travel further afield than usual, live together for some weeks or months, and spend most of their time trying to achieve their objectives. Such enterprises are of particular interest for this book, since they can be useful sources of information about man's abilities in unusual environments.

Expeditions range from large and serious government-backed

projects to small groups of students wanting a semi-scientific excuse for a holiday. There are also many sorts of expeditions whose main objectives are totally non-scientific – for example, climbing a mountain or sailing round the world. These, too, may provide incidental information of great scientific interest; but that is not their purpose. Most participants are quite willing to admit it when their aims are other than scientific. For example, Robin Knox-Johnston (the first man to sail round the world without calling at any port) wrote: 'I was doing absolutely nothing to advance scientific knowledge; I would not know how to. Nothing could be learned of human endurance from my experiences that could not be learned more quickly and accurately from tests under controlled conditions. I was sailing round the world simply because I bloody well wanted to.'[6]

Such disavowals are not acceptable in all quarters. There is a school of thought which maintains that no expedition of any kind should be undertaken without some scientific purpose in mind. In mountaineering circles this heresy is known as 'Tyndallism', after the physicist who always carried his geological hammer up mountains.[7] It has been strongly criticised. For example, Tom Patey, who was himself a physician, objected to mountaineers who claimed to be climbing from some lofty scientific motive: 'By the lochside we met a large group of earnest looking men. Climbers, perhaps? Certainly not, we were assured. Their labours were only in the cause of science and their motives, unlike ours, were purely altruistic. We had indeed surprised them in the act of completing a Bathographic Survey of Lochan Coire Mhic Fhearchair . . . It only goes to show that nowadays it is impossible, even in a remote Highland corrie, to escape the march of progress. Mountaineer-scientists, tiny embryonic Slessers,[8] lurk behind every chockstone.' Patey was not fond of mountaineering-psychologists, either: 'One recent expedition included a psychologist, whose job was to study the reaction of fellow members to stress and high altitude. Many interesting data came to light. I still feel it would have been better to study the various individual reactions to sharing camp six with a snow-goggled psychologist. It is difficult to imagine a situation more loaded with potential emotional trauma.'[9]

Individuals may have various motives for joining an expedition

B

(see Ch. 7 for some other motives), but the expedition as a whole must normally pursue some scientific objective if financial aid is sought. A list of some declared aims is given in Table I. This list was derived from the reports of thirteen Oxford University expeditions which operated between 1947 and 1969. Since most expeditions purported to undertake several projects, some popular types of projects were mentioned many times.[10]

TABLE I   *Aims mentioned by thirteen Oxford University expeditions between 1947 and 1969*

Aim	No. of mentions
Collection of biological specimens	27
Geological or glaciological surveys	15
Biological surveys	14
Geographical and land utilisation surveys	10
Collection of geological samples	9
Photography or filming	8
Social anthropology (customs, property, finance)	7
Meteorological data	4
Archaeological survey or excavation	4
Collection of human blood samples	4
Tape-recording music and language	3
Migration of birds and insects	2
Statistics on population and climate	1
Conifer diseases and hallucinogenic fungi	1
Measure native skin colours (permission refused!)	1
Physiological studies on expedition members	1
Climbing mountains	1
Search for missing climber, lost previous year	1

It is clear from the table that most expeditions were concerned with data-collection rather than experimentation, and with the physical environment rather than with man-in-the-environment. However, the later expeditions tended to show more human interest, and projects of all types became more clearly defined and more experimental.

The typical expedition had about five members, lasted for two or three months, and cost about £1,000. Members usually paid a personal contribution of £50, and received a subsidy of about £150 from various grants. Is such money well spent? Inevitably, some expeditions fail through incompetence or bad luck; but most achieve at least some of their objectives, and eventually publish their findings. Assuming the results to be valuable, they are acquired very cheaply: the same information collected on a commercial basis would cost several times as much, as the employees would demand a high salary and better living and working conditions. Often, of course, the initial results are not of much scientific value, having been collected in an amateur manner by inexperienced students. However, the final fruits of an expedition may take years to mature: plans may be laid for better projects, and students may be fired with enthusiasm for a research career. These results are hard to demonstrate, and are often ignored when evaluating the worth of expeditions.

Expeditions are often devalued not for their achievements but for their motives. Sedentary academics suspect that the expedition members are really going off 'for fun', and resent the idea that anyone should 'have a holiday and call it work'. The most irritating aspect of this criticism is the holier-than-thou assumption of the laboratory-scientist that his motives are pure while those of the expedition-scientist are not. Does he himself not work for fame or money, or for the pleasures of the academic life? His achievements may be none the worse for that. Motives have never been a reliable guide to the value of an enterprise, and no research should be judged on that basis.

III *The Social Psychology of Expeditions*

The chances of an expedition achieving its objectives are much reduced if the members do not get on well together, or are unwilling to carry out their duties. For this reason their personalities and social interactions are often studied by psychologists – an activity which is usually resented by the non-psychologists, particularly if it appears to interfere with the main objective.

Difficulties of social interaction become acute when any small and isolated group is forced to live in confined quarters for a while. Astronauts, aquanauts, lighthouse keepers, submariners,

weather-bound expeditions, and many other groups, are compelled to have less privacy and more social interaction than in
normal life. They may also suffer from lack of exercise, poor
sleep, poor or monotonous food, lack of interesting activities,
and the repetitive conversations of their companions. The usual
result is that they become excessively irritated by each other's
speech and mannerisms, and may argue about such trivialities
as whether one should say 'bacon and eggs' or 'eggs and
bacon'.[11] A partial solution to these difficulties can be found
in rigid territorial behaviour, and careful timing of activities, so
as to avoid interactions between 'incompatible' people.[12]

Trouble can be minimised by selecting only people with stable
and compatible personalities. Unfortunately, objective personality
tests have not proved very useful in team selection – though
they can help to weed out the least satisfactory personalities.[13]
Technical competence at the required task, previous expedition
experience, and motives for volunteering, are probably more
important than personality. For example, in a study of the
U.S. Navy Sealab II project (which involved living in an underwater laboratory at a depth of twenty metres), Radloff and
Helmreich[14] found that the more successful divers tended to be
older, to have had more diving experience, and to share the
motivational interests of the other divers. There were some
motivational conflicts between different groups of divers: the
Navy divers were more concerned with the practical and financial
aspects of the enterprise, while the civilian scientists were
interested in aesthetic and scientific ends.

Divergent motivation and incompatible aims are the down-
fall of many an expedition. Trouble often arises when there are
two classes of membership – 'leaders' and 'servants'. It is
scarcely surprising if the 'servants' are lazier and more mer-
cenary than the leaders, since they gain little credit for the
success of the enterprise; better work is usually obtained from
enthusiastic volunteers than from paid employees. Competition
between groups can also cause trouble, particularly when the
groups represent different nationalities. Mountaineering expeditions are especially susceptible to international rivalry, since
only a few members of the team can hope to reach the summit,
and the rest must act as servants.[15] Moreover, top climbers are

notoriously self-assertive, and even anti-social.[16] Lack of understanding of one another's language and customs exacerbates the
tensions. Members may lapse into sullen silence, when good-
natured banter, or even hot-tempered swearing, might have done
more to improve morale.[17]

A different type of rivalry can arise from mixing the sexes.
Many tales have been told of husband-swapping, broken
marriages, and sexual jealousies.[18] However, there have also
been many harmonious and successful mixed expeditions, which
escape the public eye. The presence of women can be a positive
advantage, as Sir Francis Galton pointed out: 'A woman will
endure a long journey nearly as well as a man, and certainly
better than a horse or bullock. They are invaluable in picking up
and retailing information and hearsay gossip, which will give
clues to much of importance, that, unassisted, you might miss.'[18]
Women's Liberationists may think that women can play more
important roles on expeditions; they will not pleased to learn
that (according to Taylor[18]) all-female expeditions are doomed
to be inferior to all-male ones because 'the evidence about the
behaviour of women in penal institutions (a not too dissimilar
psychological situation from Antarctica) indicates that women
do not maintain the same integrity, efficiency, and group cohesion
as men'. Fortunately, the sort of women who organise their own
expeditions bear little similarity to the sort who land up in
prison; female expeditions may be rare, but there is no evidence
to suggest that they are unsuccessful.

IV The Field Tradition in Psychology

There has never been a strong 'field' tradition within academic
psychology. 'Natural philosophers' and 'natural historians' have
always accepted the need to study natural phenomena in their
natural surroundings; but 'mainstream' psychologists have been
so concerned to establish the scientific respectability of their
discipline that they have concentrated most of their efforts upon
the powerful technique of the laboratory experiment. They
regard Fechner and Wundt as the founding fathers of modern
experimental psychology, and pay little respect to the observational and applied tradition of Galton and others.[19]

Yet the experimental method is not enough. Content and applications matter too. Laboratory experiments run the risk of sterility and irrelevance, because the phenomena which they study may never occur except in the laboratory situation. This may not matter to those who are mainly concerned with the academic excellence of their methods and theories; but it does matter to those who are curious about the 'real world', or who want their findings to be useful. For this reason there has always been a subsidiary tradition – particularly in Britain – of field studies, and of other types of applied psychology.

Francis Galton, much influenced by the ideas and methods of his cousin Charles Darwin, was one of the first psychologists to make naturalistic observations about human abilities, and to show an interest in the improvement of the human race. The psycho-anthropological tradition was boosted in the 1890s by the Cambridge University Expedition to the Torres Straits (New Guinea), in which the psychologists Rivers, Myers and McDougall went with the anthropologist Haddon to observe, measure and test the natives. Their work included tests of sensory discrimination and of susceptibility to geometrical illusions. Since then many cross-cultural studies have been carried out on sensation, perception, intellect and personality, to see how far these factors are affected by culture, race or the physical environment.[20] Much of this work was motivated by genuine curiosity about the relative importance of genetic and environmental influences on human behaviour; but much, one suspects, for political reasons. Many people would like to have 'scientific evidence' to back up their opinions that there are, or are not, important inherited differences between racial groups. However, the question remains controversial: reliable racial differences are hard to demonstrate, and harder still to interpret.

The need for the field approach has always been implicitly recognised by applied psychologists working on clinical, educational, industrial, architectural, and other social problems. They realise that behaviour in the natural setting may be quite different from behaviour in the psychological laboratory, and must be studied in its own right. This point has been argued explicitly in recent years by those who call themselves 'environmental', 'ecological' or 'naturalistic' psychologists.[21]

Much of the material in this book is drawn from the military traditions of aerospace and naval research, and the similar civilian-based research on human factors in travel on land.[22] The aim of such research is usually practical – to improve the performance of the man-machine system. Researchers often use laboratory simulations, because they are cheaper and safer than the real thing; but they are usually willing to admit that their findings may not apply in the real world, because they have failed to simulate some crucial physical or motivational variable. Consequently these researchers also rely heavily on naturalistic experiments and observations.[14]

Within the context of academic experimental psychology, there have been some theoreticians whose thinking has been wider than the laboratory. Egon Brunswik developed a theory of 'probabilistic functionalism' or 'ecological cue validity', in which he emphasised that people learn to interpret perceptual cues in the way that most often proves correct in the environment they encounter. Perception is thus more accurate in surroundings rich in natural cues than it is in an artificial and impoverished laboratory, or in any unfamiliar environment. Brunswik was one of the first to attempt to measure the ecological validity of various distance cues in the natural environment, and to obtain perceptual judgements under natural conditions.[23] This tradition has been carried on by many others – most notably by J. J. Gibson.[24] He differs from Brunswik on theoretical grounds, maintaining that the meaning of the environmental cues is inherent in the structure of the stimulation, and is somehow 'given' directly rather than learned by association. Nevertheless, his preference for the natural environment over the laboratory is similar to that of Brunswik.

This book follows the same tradition, except that the emphasis is on the errors that people make in unfamiliar environments, rather than upon the accuracy and facility with which they perceive their normal environment. Perceptual errors are often only temporary, since man can learn to reinterpret the cues with remarkable rapidity. However, there are certain physical or biological limits to human adaptability, which restrict his efficiency in some environments. The next chapter is mainly concerned with these limitations.

NOTES

1   K. Popper, *The Logic of Scientific Discovery*, London: Hutchinson, 1959.
2   D. D. Jensen, 'Paramecia, planaria, and pseudo-learning' in *Learning and Associated Phenomena in Invertebrates* (Animal Behaviour Supplement 1) edited by W. H. Thorpe and D. Davenport, London: Ballière, Tindall and Cassell, 1964.
3   A. Abramovitz and C. M. Abramovitz, 'Psychopathologies: syndromes of an ailing profession', *Bull. Brit. Psychol. Soc.*, 1970, Vol. 23, pp. 197–203.
4   T. S. Kuhn, *The Structure of Scientific Revolutions*, Chicago: Chicago University Press, 1962.
5   A notable example of the success of the 'open' approach was the discovery of the structure of DNA (the 'genetic code') by Crick and Watson; see J. D. Watson, *The Double Helix*, London: Weidenfeld & Nicolson, 1968.
6   R. Knox-Johnston, *A World of My Own*, London: Cassell, 1970.
7   John Tyndall (1820–93) was a mountaineer and a distinguished natural philosopher of varied interests. He wrote many books on mountaineering, geology, and physics.
8   Malcolm Slesser, another geologist and mountaineer, and author of several books on mountaineering, and politics.
9   T. Patey, *One Man's Mountains*, London: Gollancz, 1971, pp. 55 and 228.
10 The objectives were derived from *The Bulletin of the Oxford University Exploration Club*, 1947–69.
11 F. Spencer Chapman, *Watkins' Last Expedition*, London: Chatto and Windus, 1934, pp. 107–8.
12 I. Altman and W. H. Haythorn, 'The ecology of isolated groups', *Behavioural Science*, 1967, Vol. 12, pp. 169–82.
13 A. J. W. Taylor, 'Ability, stability and social adjustment among Scott base personnel, Antarctica', *Occupational Psychology*, 1969, Vol. 43, pp. 81–93.
14 R. Radloff and R. Helmreich, *Groups Under Stress*, New York: Appleton-Century-Crofts, 1968.
15 D. Scott, 'To rest is not to conquer', *Mountain*, 1972, Vol. 23, pp. 10–18.
16 D. Gray, 'Personality and climbing', *British Alpine Journal*, 1968, Vol. 73, pp. 167–72; J. T. Lester, 'Personality and Everest', *British Alpine Journal*, 1969, Vol. 74, pp. 101–7.
17 H. E. Ross, 'Patterns of swearing', *Discovery*, November 1960, pp. 479–81.
18 F. Galton, *The Art of Travel; or, Shifts and Contrivances available in Wild Countries*, London: Murray, 1872, p. 7 (reprinted by David and Charles at Newton Abbot, 1971).
19 For a discussion of the different traditions within psychology see E. G. Boring, *A History of Experimental Psychology*, New York: Appleton-Century-Crofts, 1957.

20 Recent reviews of the literature can be found in J. L. M. Dawson, 'Theory and research in cross-cultural psychology', *Bull. Brit. Psychol. Soc.*, 1971, Vol. 24, pp. 291–306; B. B. Lloyd, *Perception and Cognition: a cross-cultural perspective*, Harmondsworth: Penguin Books, 1972.

21 See, for example, R. G. Barker, 'Explorations in ecological psychology', *American Psychologist*, 1965, Vol. 20, pp. 1–14; E. P. Williams and H. L. Rausch (eds), *Naturalistic Viewpoints in Psychological Research*, New York: Holt, Rinehart and Winston, 1969; H. M. Proshansky, W. H. Ittelson and L. G. Rivlin (eds), *Environmental Psychology: Man and his physical setting*, New York: Holt, Rinehart and Winston, 1970.

22 There is a vast amount of government-sponsored research on these matters, often published only as laboratory reports. This material can be traced through such books as I. P. Howard and W. B. Templeton, *Human Spatial Orientation*, London: Wiley, 1966; E. C. Poulton, *Environment and Human Efficiency*, Springfield, Illinois: C. C. Thomas, 1970; C. J. Lambertsen (ed.), *Underwater Physiology*, New York: Academic Press, 1971.

23 For some of Brunswik's writings, and some essays on Brunswik's theoretical approach, see K. R. Hammond (ed.), *The Psychology of Egon Brunswik*, New York: Holt, Rinehart and Winston, 1966.

24 J. J. Gibson, *The Senses Considered as Perceptual Systems*, Boston: Houghton Mifflin Company, 1966.

CHAPTER 2

Some Limits to
Survival and Performance

Man has evolved to live on the surface of the earth, and his life is threatened if he moves into a hostile environment such as the surface of the moon or the depths of the sea. He must either adapt physiologically to the new conditions, or carry a more favourable environment with him. This chapter is concerned with the limits to adaptation, and with the ways in which efficiency is reduced in unfavourable environments.

I   Gases at Varied Pressures

An adequate supply of air is one of the most important factors in survival, and one which is much affected by changes in pressure above and below sea level. Air is normally composed of about 21 per cent oxygen (the life-supporting element), 78 per cent nitrogen, and small amounts of carbon dioxide and other gases. The volume of a gas is inversely proportional to the pressure upon it; so when the pressure is reduced the air becomes 'rarified', the gas molecules being spread more thinly in a given volume of air. Conversely, when the pressure is increased the molecules become more concentrated.

The pressure of the atmosphere at sea level is taken as equal to one bar, or one atmosphere.[1] This pressure is reduced to a half at a height of about 5,000 metres, to a tenth at about 16,000 m, and eventually to zero in outer space. Breathing becomes impossible at about 16,000 m, because the air cells in the lungs cannot absorb the oxygen molecules at such low pressure. Climbers hoping to reach the top of the highest mountains (around 9,000 m) must breath compressed air or oxygen, to obtain an adequate supply of oxygen for their needs. Similar considerations apply to balloonists and pilots flying at great heights. Most planes have pressurised cabins to maintain the air supply at approximately one bar; while spaceships are generally maintained at a lower pressure with a correspondingly higher proportion of oxygen. The extra oxygen carries the risk of an explosion, and this risk has to be measured against the increased cost of strengthening the cabin walls in order to raise the pressure. Various combinations of pressures and gas mixtures can be used, all carrying different risks and advantages.[2]

If a mountaineer – or any other traveller – stays for some time at a high altitude without an artificial air supply, he is liable to suffer from some form of 'mountain sickness' or 'altitude sickness'. The symptoms can occur at heights of 2,500 m, but do not usually become serious until much higher. The sickness is due to an inadequate supply of oxygen to the body tissues, causing vomiting and weakness. Travellers often suffer from an 'acute' attack of the sickness after a rapid increase of height, but generally recover after a day or two; others develop 'chronic' sickness, and are forced to descend to lower altitudes. Pneumonia (fluid in the lungs) and thrombosis (blood clots) are more dangerous effects of high altitude, which often prove fatal. Blood clots are actually the result of an *adaptive* thickening of the blood, the number of red blood cells increasing in order to carry more oxygen. For the same purpose there is also an increase in the oxygen-carrying capacity of the blood cells, in blood volume, in the size of the heart, and in the rate and depth of breathing.

The maximum adaptation, or acclimatisation, takes place if the traveller spends several months at about 5,000 m. Acclimatisation is probably only partial,[3] and 'high altitude deterioration' sets in above 5,500 m. Man can live for about three months at 6,000 m without an extra supply of oxygen, though with falling efficiency.[4] At 9,000 m life is possible for only about two days. Cold and semi-starvation contribute to the deterioration – the latter being due to poor appetite, and to the difficulties of preparing adequate meals during mountaineering expeditions.[5]

The discussion so far has been concerned mainly with the effects of reduced pressure at high altitudes. Beneath sea level, the increased pressure produces a different set of problems, which affect SCUBA divers, caisson workers, and anyone living in an underwater house or vehicle where the air pressure is allowed to vary with the surrounding water pressure. The pressure increases by 1 bar for every 10 m of water, being 1 b at the surface, 2 b at 10 m, 3 b at 20 m, and so on. This means that the pressure doubles between the surface and 10 m, and doubles again between 10 and 30 m, the rate of change decreasing as the diver descends. The greatest rate of change is near the surface, where the pressure doubles in 10 m – this is very large compared to the changes in the atmosphere, where it is necessary to ascend 5,000 m before the pressure halves.

Sudden large changes in pressure are hazardous. An increase of half a bar may be sufficient to burst the eardrum, if the diver is unable to equalise the pressure on both sides of the drum by opening the Eustachian tube. A decrease in pressure is much less likely to damage the drum, as the internal pressure normally opens the Eustachian tube automatically. Difficulties in equalising the pressure can cause vertigo (Ch. 6) – a symptom which is much more dangerous to aircraft pilots than to divers. One of the most dangerous aspects of the ascent for divers is the possibility of a burst lung: the reduced pressure causes the air in the lungs to expand, and, if the diver holds his breath or has a weak patch in his lungs, the air may break through the lining. This often leads to an 'air embolism' (air bubbles becoming lodged in vital tissues such as the heart), and to death.

A better-known decompression hazard is 'the bends'. This is due mainly to the nitrogen which is absorbed in the body tissues under pressure, but which reappears as bubbles when the pressure is reduced too quickly. This causes pains in the joints, sometimes followed by permanent paralysis. If the bubbles reach the heart or brain, the result may be fatal.

The bends can be avoided if the diver ascends sufficiently slowly to allow the nitrogen to leave the tissues without forming bubbles. The longer and deeper a diver stays down, the more nitrogen his tissues absorb, up to the point where they become saturated. The necessity for lengthy decompression stops puts practical limits on deep diving operations – though divers vary in the risks they are prepared to take (Ch. 7). A time-saving solution (though expensive on hardware and supporting facilities) is 'saturation diving': divers live in an underwater house at the depth at which they are required to work, and emerge for lengthy work periods. They live at constant pressure until the work is done, and are then gradually decompressed. In this way the ratio of underwater working time to decompression time is greatly increased.

All the hazards of rapid decompression which affect divers can also affect the inhabitants of planes and spacecrafts, if the pressure maintenance suddenly fails. For example, three Russian cosmonauts died in 1971 when their craft, Soyuz II, developed a leaky hatch on returning to earth. They were not wearing protective space-suits, and are said to have died of massive air-embolism.

Divers are faced with an additional disadvantage: some gases become poisonous under high pressure. Oxygen, for example, can cause convulsions at a partial pressure of more than about 1·75 b. This limits the use of pure oxygen to a depth of about 8 m, and compressed air to about 80 m (though successful air dives have been made to 120 m). Air mixtures for use at deeper depths must contain a reduced proportion of oxygen. Nitrogen is also harmful under pressure, causing 'nitrogen narcosis' or 'rapture of the deep'. Divers vary in their susceptibility, but frequently become affected below 30 m. They become euphoric, stupid, forgetful and careless – as if under the influence of alcohol. Below 130 m narcosis may cause loss of consciousness. The usual solution to this problem is to breathe an oxyhelium mixture, in which the nitrogen has been replaced by helium. Helium has very little narcotic effect, but it does have other disadvantages: it makes speech difficult (Ch. 4), it makes the diver cold, it has special decompression requirements, and it is very expensive. Nevertheless, its use is essential at great depths. Oxyhelium mixtures have been used for simulated dives in pressure chambers at pressures equivalent to below 600 m, and the limits are not yet known.

Most of the hazards mentioned so far do not apply to snorkel divers, who hold their breath for a minute or two while under water. Many diving mammals can go to great depths and stay submerged for long periods; they achieve this by a reflex submergence-syndrome, in which the heart-rate drops, circulation is restricted, and breathing is inhibited. Man shows a similar (though smaller) reflex when his face is submerged, but its form becomes modified as he learns to dive with larger lungfuls of air. The main danger for snorkelers is that they may learn to suppress the breathing reflex to such an extent that they become unconscious through lack of oxygen before surfacing. Man cannot hope to compete with porpoises, but pearl-divers frequently descend to 30 m, and the snorkel record is said to be 90 m.

II Anxiety, Narcosis and Performance

It is obvious from the previous section that pressure changes place many restrictions on a man's activities above and below sea-level. His anxiety about his own safety may add to his difficulties, reducing his efficiency at many tasks. To complicate the picture, a diver's efficiency may be further reduced if he is sufficiently deep to be affected by nitrogen narcosis.

It is hard to specify the effects of narcosis on performance, because it is difficult to run a well-controlled experiment. There are large differences between subjects; there are safety restrictions on the order in which tests can be run; it is difficult to prevent subjects from knowing what depth they are at; and there are interactions with cold, anxiety and other factors. Many experiments have been carried out in pressure chambers, partially simulating the effects of deep diving.[6] They show that narcosis has a harmful effect on both manual dexterity and reasoning, but mainly on reasoning.

Anxiety is not a variable that is easy to define or measure. It is not an environmental variable, like a change in temperature or light intensity. It is a mental and physiological reaction to a dangerous or stressful situation. Since it is hard to find situations that are stressful to all subjects, the existence of anxiety has to be inferred from physiological or behavioural evidence, or believed from introspective reports. Anxiety thus has the status of an 'intervening variable' in psychological theory: it cannot be measured directly, but it fills an explanatory gap between other variables which can be measured. For example, Weltman, Christianson and Egstrom[7] took physiological measures from divers who were carrying out a construction task at a depth of six m in the sea and in a water tank. The breathing and heart rate increased significantly for the novice divers in the sea, as did the time to complete the construction task. The experienced divers showed no significant differences between the tank and the sea on any measure. The most reasonable explanation is that the novices became anxious in the sea, and that this interfered with their performance.

Anxiety is also a useful explanatory concept to account for the fact that pressure chamber experiments on nitrogen narcosis sometimes fail to replicate the effects found at equivalent depths in the sea. For example, Baddeley and his colleagues[6] found that in 'safe' water close to the shore, performance was similar to that in a pressure chamber; but that in open water it deteriorated much more rapidly with increasing depth. They concluded that the anxiety induced by being deep and far from shore interacted with narcosis to produce an exaggerated decrement in performance.

A curious symptom said to occur under narcosis, drunkenness, schizophrenia, anxiety and many other forms of stress is 'tunnel vision' or 'perceptual narrowing'. This is sometimes described in dramatic terms as a loss of peripheral vision, accompanied by distortions of apparent size and distance. However, there is little experimental evidence for a large change in the visual field; rather, there seems to be a lack of attention to peripheral objects, or a redistribution of attention over the visual field. Ross and Rejman[8] found no clear evidence of perceptual narrowing when testing naval divers in a pressure chamber at sixty m, though there was a trend towards lowered attention over the whole visual field. Better evidence for perceptual narrowing has been found in anxiety-provoking situations: Weltman and his colleagues were able to demonstrate its occurrence in novice divers at a depth of 8 m in the open sea,[9] and also at a *simulated* depth of 20 m in a pseudo-pressure-chamber experiment.[10] In the latter experiment the novices were tricked into believing that the pressure was being increased, by much hissing of air and by false readings on the pressure gauge. This was sufficient to cause raised heart rates for most subjects throughout the experiment, and some reports of anxiety. Visual tests showed central acuity to be unimpaired, while there was a marked drop in the detection rate for peripheral signals. The most probable explanation is that subjects redistribute their attention under stress, concentrating mainly on the most important aspect of the task – which usually coincides with the centre of the visual field.

There are many other activities which are at least as dangerous as diving. Parachute jumping, rock-climbing and war are obvious examples; but they are more difficult to investigate. One cannot perform a card-sorting experiment half way up a rock face, or distract a soldier who is busy defusing a bomb. It is sometimes possible to monitor physiological changes during such activities, but behavioural tests must usually be restricted to the periods before and after the stressful activity. Various experimenters have tried to get round some of these difficulties by simulating dangerous events while testing their subjects.[11] The simulations frequently fail, as subjects naturally believe that little harm will come to them while taking part in a psychological experiment. Extreme simulations such as a threatened plane crash[12] may be successful, but the morality of such experiments is questionable.

It is hardly surprising that most experiments show some type of decrement at skilled tasks during dangerous activities. However, there are various theories which could account for this.[13] One universal type of psychological theory is described by a hump-shaped curve. When it is applied to the effects of stress on performance, it is generally known as the Yerkes-Dodson Law. It states that performance is best when the subject is moderately aroused, and deteriorates under low or high arousal (Fig. 2.1). The optimum level of arousal is also said to vary with the difficulty of the task, being lower for more complex tasks: it is best to be highly anxious to win a fruit-picking competition, but to face a university examination with equanimity. One difficulty with this theory is that it is so flexible that it can

PLATE 1

Targets for a distance-judgement test under water, at Wied-iż-Żurrieq,
Malta. The furthest targets, at 25 m, are scarcely visible due to loss of
contrast. (Photograph by J. N. Lythgoe. From H. E. Ross, *Underwater
Assoc. Rep. Malta, 1965, pp. 19–22.*)

PLATE 2

Brocken spectre of three figures surrounded by a halo. Looking down to a cloudbank from Tower Ridge, Ben Nevis, Scotland. (Photograph by P. Murray-Rust.)

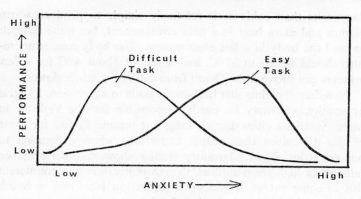

FIGURE 2.1
Relation between performance, task-difficulty and anxiety.

account for almost anything; also, it seems most appropriate to those situations where the subject's anxiety is closely related to the outcome of the task, and he is highly motivated to perform well. However, in many dangerous situations the subject is more anxious about his own survival than he is about the task. A threat to survival is a *distractor*, and will normally worsen performance unless the task is directly related to survival.

In moments of great danger it is natural to concentrate upon the method of escape; but this concentration may not always be beneficial. The panic-stricken man may continue with an inappropriate action, instead of looking for a new method of escape: drivers have been known to sit in their stalled cars on a level-crossing, repeatedly pressing the starter button until the train arrives, when they should have engaged first gear or got out and run. One of the reasons why the experienced individual is so much more efficient than the novice is that he is less anxious. He knows what to do in an emergency, and is far less likely to panic if anything begins to go wrong.

III *Temperature*

Extremes of temperature are a common source of death or discomfort, both for the explorers of strange environments and for those who live in intemperate zones. Heat is normally more dangerous than cold: it is relatively simple to produce warm clothes and extra heat in a cold environment, but quite difficult to cool the body in a hot environment. The body core temperature should be about 37°C, and a rise of about 4°C for a few minutes can prove fatal. Death from cooling is much slower.

Wyndham[14] claims that heat-stress leads to aggression, hysteria or apathy, and may be partly responsible for the violence in some American cities during 'long, hot summers', and for some of the difficulties that people experience when emigrating to hot countries. Most laboratory studies show that performance falls off in high temperatures, though motivation can counteract this to some extent. Wyndham's studies on labourers in South African gold mines show that fatal heat-stroke rarely occurs below effective temperatures of 25·5°C, but increases thereafter. He also found that the degree of acclimatisation was more important than racial origin in the ability to withstand heat.

Heat can be a severe problem in hot climates and in certain enclosed environments, but cold is the main enemy up mountains and under water. Wet-cold is more dangerous than dry-cold, so more people die in Britain from hypothermia than might be expected from the temperature alone. Cold combined with wind is also more dangerous than cold alone. Low temperature, wind, rain and snow are common on the higher British mountains, leading to exposure and sometimes to frostbite. When a person becomes cold, the blood supply to the outer parts of the body is reduced in order to protect the inner core. If the inner core begins to cool, hypothermia sets in and death may occur. The chance of this happening is increased by fatigue, anxiety and general inexperience. Men are more susceptible than women, and children than adults. Hill walkers are at risk even when adequately clothed, as they tend to sweat as they climb: they then cool down rapidly in their damp clothing if they stop for a rest, or if the weather deteriorates. Some behavioural symptoms of the early stages of exposure are lack of self-control, low morale, paranoia, and poor memory. If the sufferer is forced to carry on, his condition may deteriorate – but carrying on may be safer than resting in an exposed place in wet clothing.

The lower susceptibility of experienced climbers is probably both physiological and psychological. The psychological advantage is the knowledge that they or their peers have survived similar conditions in the past – they suffer less anxiety, and fewer of the physiological problems which can result from anxiety. They also undergo some physiological adaptation, or acclimatisation, as a result of repeated exposure to cold. Acclimatisation seems to be like other sorts of learning, in that it is not entirely 'forgotten' when the climate changes. It occurs more quickly on subsequent exposures than on the first exposure. In fact it is possible for the same person to become acclimatised to both heat and cold, and to be able to cope with either extreme.[14] The experienced traveller probably learns to produce the appropriate physiological response, since it is rewarding to do so. It is now clear that many autonomic responses can be brought under voluntary control by operant conditioning procedures:[15] it is possible that the same applies to acclimatisation. Anxious people seem to suffer more from the cold than relaxed people. This may be because they are less likely to show a good vasodilation response when cold.[16] Vasodilation is a reflex response to initial chilling below about 12°C, which allows the blood to flow faster and thus helps to keep the patient warm. This is followed by vasoconstriction before the inner core temperature drops.

Cold water is much more chilling than cold air, as heat passess easily from the body to the water. The heat balance of an unclothed swimmer cannot usually be maintained in water below about 20°C; and if the water is near freezing, death will occur in under an hour. However, very fat men can survive almost indefinitely in water over 12°C. (This is one of the few circumstances in which it is better to be fat than thin!) The temperature on the continental shelf varies between about 7–13°C, so divers in these waters must wear adequate suits (preferably heated) if they are to work satisfactorily for any length of time. A conventional neoprene wet-suit will not keep a diver very warm at depth, because the pressure squashes the air cells in the suit. However, on the surface a wet-suit can enable a swimmer to survive almost indefinitely in British waters – one lost diver survived sixteen and a half hours in water of 12°C.[17]

A large number of studies has been conducted on the effects

of cold on performance, mainly in air[11] rather than water. Performance at most tasks deteriorates in the cold, but this is mainly due to the fact that the fingers become numb when the skin temperature drops below 13°C. However, it is possible that sensations of cold also affect central processes in the brain, since Lockhart[18] has shown that performance deteriorates when the hands are warm but the body-skin is cold. Every diver knows that his thoughts become sluggish towards the end of a cold dive, but there is very little experimental evidence to support this idea. Stang and Wiener[19] found that performance at manual tasks declined with body temperature in cold water. Reaction time in a 'choice' situation also deteriorated, but mental arithmetic was unaffected. Bowen[20] obtained similar results, with only slight trends towards a deterioration of reasoning tasks when cold. Bowen suggested that cold might act as a distractor, and thus interfere with memory and attention for complex tasks. Some evidence for this was found by Weltman and his colleagues;[21] non-mathematical divers performed worse on problem-solving tasks when cold, while mathematically-trained subjects were unaffected. Baddeley[22] also found some impairment of memory for items learned in cold water and recalled thirty minutes later in the warmth on land; but he found no impairment on reasoning tests in cold water, and no drop in the detection of peripheral visual signals. He suggested that divers might lack the motivation to learn when cold; or that there might be a 'surroundings' effect, memory being best when tested under similar conditions to the learning situation. The body temperature of the divers in these experiments did not drop more than about 1°C, and it is possible that greater temperature losses are necessary before much mental deterioration can be demonstrated experimentally. However, there are difficulties in obtaining volunteers for this sort of experiment!

Divers who make a practice of diving in cold water show some evidence of physiological acclimatisation.[23] They can also learn to preserve their heat by breathing more slowly: 30 per cent of the heat loss is caused by breathing-in cold air. It is quite probable that their performance at skilled tasks would also show less deterioration than that of unacclimatised divers, but this does not seem to have been investigated.

IV *Sleep Disturbances and Time Estimation*

Travel to foreign parts, or a change of life-style, tends to disrupt normal sleep habits. This makes most people tired and irritable – and less efficient at certain types of task, unless they try hard to compensate for their tiredness.[24]

The total amount of sleep is not the only important factor: there are different types of sleep, and it is possible to become deficient in one type only. Shift workers and poor sleepers, for example, tend to lack REM (dreaming) sleep, while the depressed and elderly tend to lack Stage 4 (deep) sleep. People can acquire 'debts' for the various sorts of sleep, and make them up when allowed.[25] A further problem is that even though a normal number of hours is spent in sleep, the sleep may be taken at the 'wrong' time of day. Sleep patterns, body temperature and various other bodily functions show regular *circadian rhythms* – fluctuations over the twenty-four hours of a day/night cycle. Efficiency at mental tasks varies throughout the twenty-four hours, and is normally highest when body temperature is highest (around 8.00 p.m.) and lowest when temperature is lowest (around 4–5.00 a.m.). If people are forced to be awake at times when they would normally be asleep, they become irritable and inefficient. This may be one reason why people who appear to be taking adequate total sleep, but at irregular intervals, complain of insufficient sleep.[26]

Circadian rhythms are usually entrained to the normal twenty-four-hour cycle by various *Zeitgebers* (time-givers), such as the light/dark cycle and social factors. In night-shift work there is a conflict between the social and physical *Zeitgebers*, but most people's bodily rhythms adjust to the new régime within about a week. Flying to a new country through several time zones is similar to going on night-shift, except that the *Zeitgebers* all coincide in the new country. There is some uncertainty as to whether eastward or westward flights cause more disruption. Experimental studies vary as to whether the flights are by day or night, whether the subjects are leaving or returning home, and whether there is a change of climate and social requirements. Various simulations have been carried out in 'bunker' experiments, in which subjects are kept under artificial light, and the light/dark cycles are changed experimentally. These studies suggest that adaptation is faster in an eastward direction – when subjects have to get up and go to sleep earlier than usual. Real flight studies tend to show better westward adjustment. The latter finding tends to fit common experience with small time shifts, such as the hour's difference between Greenwich Mean Time and Summer Time: most people dislike rising early, but have no objection to sleeping late. In winter there is an additional problem – the difficulty of waking up when it is still dark. This was one of the reasons for the unpopularity of the experiment with British Standard Time (perpetual Summer Time) – it was all right for London businessmen, but not for early workers or the Celtic fringes.

If a person is kept in isolation in continuous light or darkness without any information about the time, it is possible to study his biological rhythms unentrained to any known *Zeitgebers*. Michel Siffre,[27] the French speleologist, undertook an experiment of this sort. He spent sixty-three days alone in a cave at a depth of 114 m below the Maritime Alps. His cycle increased to about twenty-four and a half hours, though he believed it to be much less. Other people subsequently stayed for longer periods in caves, including David Lafferty in the Cheddar caves in 1966 for 127 days. Jean-Paul Mairetet[28] later spent 174 days in a cave at a depth of 70 m. He soon switched to a cycle with thirty-two hours of wakefulness and fourteen of sleep, keeping up this rhythm for forty-eight actual days. The other biological rhythms became out of phase with this sleep cycle, and he showed a lengthened reaction time on psychological tests. He then reverted to a normal circadian rhythm for the remaining days. Other authors have also found evidence of *internal desynchronisation* (different biological functions becoming out of phase) during free-running bunker experiments.[28] Lewis and Lobban[29] observed the same effect in subjects who were kept on artificial twenty-one- or twenty-seven-hour cycles in Spitzbergen, during the continuous light of the Arctic summer. It appears that though the sleep cycle can be altered in length, the other rhythms cannot deviate far from twenty-four hours. Large changes result in desynchronisation, and thus cause inefficiency. There is no chance, then, that man could ever adapt to the lunar day, which lasts a terrestrial month.

Caves do not provide the best environment for running scientific experiments, and the participants are often more concerned with breaking endurance records than with providing reliable data. However, many well-controlled bunker experiments have provided additional data on free-running rhythms. They show some large individual differences, but most subjects adopt a rhythm of about twenty-five hours. This seems to suggest either that a twenty-five-hour rhythm is 'natural' (but why?); or that the twenty-four-hour internal clock tends to run slow unless entrained.

A few observational studies have been made of the sleep patterns of members of expeditions. Lewis and Masterton[30] found that members of a Greenland expedition took an average of 7·9 hours sleep, with little difference between summer and winter. Ross[26] found an average of 7·8 hours, in the continuous summer light of northern Norway. On this expedition sleep was taken at very variable times because of scientific and other activities, but the total sleep was slightly greater than that taken at home (7·6 hours). Williams[31] found that members of a Himalayan expedition took more sleep when between 3,000–6,000 m than when below 3,000 m (7·8 as opposed to 7·0 hours). There were more interruptions, and a shift to earlier bedtimes and risings at altitude, but no loss of total sleep. Higher altitudes are probably necessary before altitude sickness causes loss of sleep.

It is sometimes claimed that changes in sleep patterns or body temperature disturb time estimation.[32] The assumption is that time perception is like a sensory process, with some 'internal clock' providing the sensory stimulation. For example, Mairetet thought his 'days' in the cave were of normal length, and was surprised to find how long he had actually spent underground. However, Siffre also underestimated his time in the cave by about half, though his cycle was almost normal. It has often been suggested that body temperature is important, the internal clock speeding up in the heat and slowing down in the cold. This might account for the apparent shortening of time (slowing down of the internal clock) in the cool caves. Baddeley[33] obtained a similar result with cold divers, when they were asked to estimate a minute. However, there are several other contradictory reports about the effects of temperature or of circadian rhythms.[32] Changes in the internal clock cannot, logically, make time appear to run at the wrong speed, unless the subject has additional information about *true* time. Other factors, such as boredom or interest, must affect the rate at which true time appears to pass. A novel task, such as a new job or journey, appears to pass slowly; while a familiar task or habitual journey passes quickly and unnoticed. On the other hand, time passes very slowly when one is waiting for a bus or listening to a boring lecture; and time flies when one is absorbed in an interesting and pleasant task. Time may also seem different depending on whether one is asked to estimate it retrospectively, or to pay attention to it while it passes. It seems unlikely that there is any unitary time sense. Rather, there are many cognitive factors which determine one's attitudes to the passing of time, and one's ability to estimate time intervals.

V Gravity, Acceleration and Buoyancy

Objects retain the same mass, or inertia, whether they are on the surface of the moon, in outer space, or under water. Nevertheless, they undergo large changes in weight, or the force required to lift them. The gravitational force on the moon is only one sixth that on earth, so astronauts can walk on its surface carrying loads that would be impossibly heavy on earth. However, since the inertial force is unchanged, a surprisingly large effort is required to start or stop movements, which is why astronauts 'walk' in a series of slow jumps. During most of the space-flight astronauts are weightless, owing to zero gravity, and can float inside or outside the space-craft.[2, 11] Their own inertia makes it difficult for them to stop, and they are liable to crash into surrounding objects. They also have difficulty in applying torque, since the force tends to push their body away from the object.

Zero gravity has another disadvantage – it is a hazard to health. Prolonged weightlessness causes a loss of weight, of red blood cells, and of minerals from the bones, and a weakening of the cardiovascular system. This is not too troublesome during the space-flight, but astronauts tend to feel weak for some time after returning to normal gravity. The risk of death or damage from this cause is one of the obstacles to longer space-flights.

On earth, objects are normally lifted against the force of the earth's gravity (1 g). If they are lifted against an additional accelerative force, they become heavier. Travellers are subjected to accelerative forces during changes in the motion of the vehicle. Acceleration is especially violent at the start and finish of a space journey. During lift-off, the force increases from 1 g to 7 g in five minutes; and during re-entry there is a decelerative force (negative acceleration) of the same size. People become very clumsy under increased g, as it is difficult to move the limbs against the direction of the force. Similarly, the blood circulation slows down, because of the effective increase in the weight of the blood. At 5 g, footward ('eyeballs up') acceleration causes blackout, and headward ('eyeballs down') causes 'redout'. The astronaut is normally seated in the spacecraft so that the force acts in an 'eyeballs-in' direction, which is the least damaging and avoids blackouts or redouts.

Zero g can be achieved for a short while during free fall, or parabolic flight, when the gravitational force and the accelerative force cancel each other. Weightlessness can be maintained for about thirty seconds during a parabolic flight, but this is always preceded and followed by a few seconds of 1–3 g. The short time period makes this method unsuitable for training astronauts in the effects of weightlessness, and various substitutes have been devised.[2] The most popular method is immersion in water.[34] Gravity operates as normal in water, but its effects can be counteracted by the upthrust of the water. Different parts of the body vary in density, but if a diver is correctly weighted to compensate for this, most of his body can be made neutrally buoyant. The neutral diver has much the same difficulties as the weightless astronaut in moving and manipulating objects, and in compensating for inertial force. Divers who wish to work effectively under water usually weight themselves down while carrying out the task. Similarly, astronauts on the moon wear heavy boots.

What happens to the *apparent* weight of an object when its effective weight is changed? And what happens to the ability to detect a change in mass or weight? The answer is quite complicated, because the weight of the arm must be considered as well as the weight of the object:[35] laboratory simulations in which only the object's weight is altered do not tell the whole story. In normal life, changes in gravity or buoyancy affect the arm as well as other objects, and the effective change in arm-weight gives the brain a cue to the weight-transformation. The result is that adaptation occurs, apparent weight reverting towards the untransformed weight. This has been demonstrated for objects in water: when swimmers first enter the water they judge objects to be considerably lighter than in air, but after ten minutes they judge them to be quite near their air-weight; and on leaving the water they suffer from a short after-effect in which objects on land feel heavier than usual.[36] Weight discrimination also deteriorates when the swimmer first enters or leaves the water, but returns to normal when time is allowed for adaptation.[37]

Under zero g all objects are weightless, so cannot be discriminated by weight. However, their mass can still be discriminated by differences in inertial force. This was shown by Rees and Copeland[38] in a simulation experiment, in which the objects rested on a cushion of air. They found that mass-discrimination was twice as poor as weight-discrimination under normal gravity. However, their procedure did not alter arm-weight. If the arm were also weightless, it is quite probable that mass-discrimination would improve.

People tend to reach too high when aiming for objects under water, or during short periods of weightlessness; and too low under 3 g upward acceleration.[11] It is not clear whether the effect is due to changed arm-weight, or to visual distortion caused by water (Ch. 3) or by changes in g (Ch. 6). In any event, the mis-reaching seems to disappear with time and practice.

VI *Visual Deterioration*

A hostile environment can cause a deterioration in sensory efficiency in two ways: it can lower the efficiency of the brain or sense organ, and it can reduce the quantity or quality of the physical stimulation reaching the sense organ. This is true of all the senses; but, since we are so dependent on vision, most research has been done on vision.

Almost any change in the environment can be shown to have a small effect on visual acuity.[11] Some of the most important environmental factors are the level of illumination, the brightness contrast between the object and its background, and the size of the image which the object subtends at the viewer's eye. Some important 'internal' variables are the accommodation of the lens, the state of light or dark adaptation, and the expectations of the viewer. Most acuity experiments have been carried out in laboratories, and they often fail to predict the level of performance in more complex situations. For example, in most tests the viewer and target are stationary, whereas in normal life one or other is frequently moving. 'Dynamic' acuity is poorer than 'static' acuity, and there is a low correlation between the two.[39] Another example is the factor of image size, and its relation to the observation distance: most laboratory experiments show that the observation distance is unimportant, acuity being determined by the *angular* size;[40] nevertheless, many 'practical' experiments show that acuity improves (in angular terms) as the target distance increases.[41-44] One possible explanation is that changes in *apparent* size can have some effect on acuity: distant objects look apparently larger than near objects of the same angular size (Ch. 3), and this may improve acuity.[45]

Experiments during parabolic flights suggest that changes in g cause a deterioration in acuity.[41, 42] However, noise, vibration and postural changes may have contributed to the effect. There is little evidence of any serious loss of acuity during weightlessness in space flight. American astronauts have reported seeing very fine details looking down to earth, and acuity tests within the spacecraft show normal vision.[2] The Russians, however, have reported difficulty in focusing and in the judgement of shape and texture, and some reduction in the apparent brightness of colours. Such disturbances are fairly trivial: cosmic rays and high levels of ultra-violet and visible light carry much greater dangers for the astronaut. Visors can protect their eyes from light rays, but not from cosmic rays.

Excessive light can also trouble skiers and winter mountaineers, causing snow-blindness if they do not wear protective goggles. Normal levels of light, too, can be damaging to potholers and others who have been dark-adapted for a long time. Light-adaptation usually occurs quickly, but it is slow after some days in the dark. The eye adapts almost instantaneously to moderate changes in illumination (such as when the sun goes behind a cloud) but takes longer for large changes. One of the difficulties of night driving is that glare from oncoming headlights spoils the driver's dark-adaptation, and thus worsens his already meagre visual acuity. The use of polarised headlights and visors could partially remove this difficulty.[46]

Dark-adaptation is a lengthy process, taking at least thirty minutes for a change from bright sunlight to dim illumination. This reduces the visual efficiency of divers entering dark water – and they may have finished the dive before their adaptation is complete. However, the canny diver can improve matters by wearing red goggles for about half an hour before the dive.[47] This hastens adaptation because the rod cells, which are used in dim light, are insensitive to red wavelengths: these cells can therefore start dark-adapting under a red filter, while the cones continue to give normal daylight vision.

A further difficulty which sometimes affects divers and pilots is 'empty-field myopia'. When there is nothing to see, the eye tends to focus at about 3 m, with the result that any object in the distance will be out of focus and may not be noticed. This makes it difficult to predict visual search performance in practical situations from normal laboratory data. Empty-field myopia is unlikely to affect astronauts, since they have the stars to look at. It is more of a nuisance in the white-out conditions that exist when flying in a cloud, walking or skiing in a snow-storm, or diving in cloudy water. It can also affect divers in clear deep water, who see nothing but a 'blue sphere' all around them.

Divers tend to suffer from poor vision for a variety of reasons. The human eye is extremely long-sighted in water, because the refractive power of the corneal surface is lost, its refractive index being almost the same as that of water. The unaided lens is unable to accommodate sufficiently to produce a clear image, and acuity is about ten times poorer than in air.[48] Sir Francis

Galton[49] invented underwater spectacles to compensate for this, but most divers wear a facemask which allows the eye to operate in air. Some divers prefer underwater contact-lenses, but these are expensive and troublesome, and leave the face unprotected from cold and other damage. The facemask is the simplest solution; but it has drawbacks such as liability to misting, restriction of peripheral vision,[6] and the introduction of optical distortion in water (Ch. 3).

The visibility of the water is often the most important factor in determining visual performance. Visibility of 30 m is considered to be a thick fog on land, but excellent under water. The visibility of British coastal waters rarely exceeds 20 m, and is often almost zero. Murky water reduces the brightness and colour contrast between an object and its background, by the absorption and scattering of light.[47] It is low contrast, rather than low illumination, that limits visibility during most shallow dives in daylight. Low contrast is probably the main reason why tests in the sea show much poorer acuity than in air, acuity deteriorating with the viewing distance.[6]

This chapter has considered some of the ways in which man's performance, and indeed his very life, is limited by hostile environments. A small degree of psychophysiological adaptation is possible, but the main advances have been made through man's ability to invent machines which make adaptation unnecessary. The later chapters are more concerned with perceptual phenomena, where machines are of little use, and illusions abound. This is particularly true of space-perception, where cues which normally have one meaning take on a new meaning in a different environment. Under these circumstances, adaptation and learning are of great importance.

NOTES

1   One bar is almost equivalent to the older unit, one atmosphere. The following values are equivalent: 1·02 bars; 1 atmosphere; 14·7 pounds per square inch; 102 kilonewtons per square metre; 760 millimetres of mercury.
2   For a very readable review, see M. R. Sharpe, *Living in Space*, London: Aldus Books Ltd., 1969.

3   E. R. Tichauer, 'Operation of machine tools at high altitudes', *Ergonomics*, 1963, Vol. 6, pp. 51–73.

4   M. B. Gill, E. C. Poulton, A. Carpenter, M. M. Woodhead and M. H. P. Gregory, 'Falling efficiency at sorting cards during acclimatization at 19,000 ft', *Nature*, 1964, Vol. 203, p. 436.

5   C. F. Consolazio, H. L. Johnson, H. J. Krzywicki and T. A. Daws, 'Metabolic aspects of acute altitude exposure (4,300 metres) in adequately nourished humans', *Amer. J. Clinical Nutrition*, 1972, Vol. 25, pp. 23–9.

6   For a review, see A. D. Baddeley, 'Diver performance', Ch. 2 in *Underwater Science*, edited by J. D. Woods and J. N. Lythgoe, London: Oxford University Press, 1971.

7   G. Weltman, R. A. Christianson and G. H. Egstrom, 'Effects of environment and experience on underwater work performance', *Human Factors*, 1970, Vol. 12, pp. 587–98.

8   H. E. Ross and M. H. Rejman, 'Narcosis and visual attention', in *Progress in Underwater Science*, edited by J. N. Lythgoe and J. D. Woods, London: Academic Press, 1974.

9   G. Weltman and G. H. Egstrom, 'Perceptual narrowing in novice divers', *Human Factors*, 1966, Vol. 8, pp. 499–506.

10 G. Weltman, J. E. Smith and G. H. Egstrom, 'Perceptual narrowing during simulated pressure-chamber exposure', *Human Factors*, 1971, Vol. 13, pp. 99–107.

11 For a review see E. C. Poulton, *Environment and Human Efficiency*, Springfield, Illinois: C. C. Thomas, 1970.

12 M. M. Berkun, H. M. Bialek, R. P. Kern and K. Yagi, 'Experimental studies of psychological stress in man', *Psychol. Monog.*, 1962, Vol. 76, (15, whole no. 534).

13 A. D. Baddeley, 'Selective attention and performance in dangerous environments', *Brit. J. Psychol.*, 1972, Vol. 63, pp. 537–46.

14 C. H. Wyndham, 'Adaptation to heat and cold', in *Physiology, Environment and Man*, edited by D. H. K. Lee and D. Minard, New York: Academic Press, 1970.

15 C. Snyder and M. Noble, 'Operant conditioning of vasoconstriction', *J. exp. Psychol.*, 1968, Vol. 77, pp. 263–8.

16 W. H. Teichner, 'Delayed cold induced vasodilation and behavior', *J. exp. Psychol.*, 1965, Vol. 69, pp. 426–32.

17 J. Bevan, 'The way to survive', *Triton*, 1972, Vol. 17, p. 93.

18 J. M. Lockhart, 'Extreme body cooling and psychomotor performance', *Ergonomics*, 1968, Vol. 11, pp. 249–60.

19 P. R. Stang and E. L. Wiener, 'Diver performance in cold water', *Human Factors*, 1970, Vol. 12, pp. 391–9.

20 H. M. Bowen, 'Diver performance and the effects of cold', *Human Factors*, 1968, Vol. 8, pp. 183–99.

21 G. Weltman, G. E. Egstrom, M. A. Willis and W. Cuccaro, 'Underwater work measurement techniques: final report', Biotech. Lab. Tech. Rep. No. 50, UCLA-ENG-7140, Dept. of Engineering, University of California at Los Angeles, July 1971.

22 A. D. Baddeley, 'The cognitive efficiency of divers in cold water', Paper read to the Underwater Association Symposium, London, 1972.

23   S. Skreslet and F. Aarefjord, 'Acclimatization to cold in man induced by frequent Scuba diving in cold water', *J. Appl. Physiol.*, 1968, Vol. 24, pp. 177–81.

24   R. T. Wilkinson, 'Sleep deprivation', in *The Physiology of Human Survival*, edited by O. G. Edholm and A. L. Bacharach, London: Academic Press, 1965.

25   G. S. Tune, 'The human sleep debt', *Science Journal*, December 1968, pp. 67–71.

26   H. E. Ross, 'Sleep and wakefulness in the Arctic under an irregular régime', in *Biometeorology: Proc. 2nd Int. Bioclimatological Congress*, edited by S. W. Tromp, Oxford: Pergamon, 1962.

27   M. Siffre, *Beyond Time*, (trans. H. Briffault), London: Chatto & Windus, 1965.

28   G. Oleron, P. Fraisse, N. Zuili and M. Siffre, 'The effects of variations in the sleep-wakefulness cycle during a "Time-Isolation" experiment on reaction time and spontaneous tempo', in *Aspects of Human Efficiency*, edited by W. P. Colquhoun, London: English Universities Press, 1972.

29   P. R. Lewis and M. C. Lobban, 'Dissociation of diurnal rhythms in human subjects living on abnormal time routines', *Quart. J. exp. Physiol.*, 1957, Vol. 42, pp. 371–86.

30   H. E. Lewis and J. P. Masterton, 'Sleep and wakefulness in the arctic', *Lancet*, 1957, Vol. 1, pp. 1262–6.

31   E. S. Williams, 'Sleep and wakefulness at high altitudes', *Brit. Med. J.*, 1959, Vol. 1, pp. 197–8.

32   For reviews of time perception see J. Cohen, *Psychological Time in Health and Disease*, Springfield, Illinois: C. C. Thomas, 1967; R. E. Ornstein, *On the Experience of Time*, Harmondsworth: Penguin Books, 1969; J. E. Orme, *Time, Experience and Behaviour*, London: Iliffe Books Ltd., 1969.

33   A. D. Baddeley, 'Reduced body temperature and time estimation', *Amer. J. Psychol.*, 1966, Vol. 79, pp. 475–9.

34   J. H. Duddy, 'The simulation of weightlessness using water immersion techniques: an annotated bibliography', *Human Factors*, 1969, Vol. 11, 507–40.

35   R. L. Gregory and H. E. Ross, 'Arm weight, adaptation and weight discrimination', *Percept. Mot. Skills*, 1967, Vol. 24, pp. 1127–30.

36   H. E. Ross, M. H. Rejman and P. Lennie, 'Adaptation to weight transformation in water', *Ergonomics*, 1972, Vol. 15, pp. 387–97.

37   H. E. Ross and M. H. Rejman, 'Weight discrimination in water', in *Science Diving International*, edited by N. C. Flemming, Andover: Standard Press, 1973, pp. 163–7.

38   D. W. Rees and N. K. Copeland, 'Discrimination of differences in mass of weightless objects', U.S.A.F. W.A.D.D. Tech. Rep. 60–601. Wright-Patterson Air Force Base, Ohio, 1960.

39   S. Weissman and C. Freeburne, 'Relationship between static and dynamic visual acuity', *J. exp. Psychol.*, 1965, Vol. 70, pp. 141–6.

40   For a review see L. L. Sloan, 'Measurement of visual acuity', *A.M.A. Arch. Ophthal.*, 1951, Vol 45, pp. 704–25.

41   W. J. White and W. R. Jorve, 'The effects of gravitational stress

upon visual acuity', W.A.D.C. Tech. Rep. 56–247. Wright-Patterson Air Force Base, Ohio, 1956.

42 L. D. Pigg and W. N. Kama, 'The effect of transient weightlessness on visual acuity', W.A.D.C. Tech. Rep. 61–184. Wright-Patterson Air Force Base, Ohio, 1961.

43 G. Amigo, 'Variation of stereoscopic acuity with observation distance', *J. opt. Soc. Amer.*, 1963, Vol. 53, pp. 630–5.

44 A. Chapanis and L. C. Scarpa, 'Readability of dials at different distances with constant visual angle', *Human Factors*, 1967, Vol. 9, pp. 419–26.

45 E. A. Alluisi, 'Measured visual acuity as a function of phenomenal size', W.A.D.C. Tech. Rep. 55–384, Wright-Patterson Air Force Base, Ohio, 1955.

46 K. Rumar, 'Effectiveness of old, new, and future motor-car lighting', *Applied Ergonomics*, 1971, Vol. 2, pp. 99–103.

47 For a review of visibility and vision under water, see J. N. Lythgoe, 'Vision', Ch. 4 in *Underwater Science*, edited by J. D. Woods and J. N. Lythgoe, London: Oxford University Press, 1971.

48 S. M. Luria and J. A. S. Kinney, 'Visual acuity underwater without a face mask', U.S.N.S.M.C. Rep. No. 581, U.S. Naval Submarine Base, Groton, Connecticut, 06340, 1969.

49 F. Galton, *The Art of Travel; or, Shifts and Contrivances available in Wild Countries*, London: Murray, 1872, p. 87 (Reprinted by David & Charles Ltd., 1971).

PLATE 3

Objects of unknown size. Early-warning station, Fylingdales, North Yorkshire Moors, England.

PLATE 4

Raised horizon and sloping water. Looking to Stàc Pollaidh from Cùl Mòr, Ross and Cromarty, Scotland. (Photograph by P. Clark.)

CHAPTER 3

Visual Environments and Spatial Perception

'Objects appear nearer than they really are: First, when the light is bright and shining on the object; secondly when looking across water or snow, or looking uphill or down. Objects appear further off when in the shade; across a valley; when the background is of the same colour; when the observer is lying down or kneeling; when there is a heat haze over the ground.' This prescription of Baden-Powell's[1] for outdoor distance estimates bears little relation to the conventional list of 'distance cues' which can be found in standard textbooks of psychology. This chapter aims to redress the balance, by concentrating mainly on the cues that occur out of doors, and which vary in different environments.

I Aerial Perspective and Brightness Contrast

The visibility of objects out of doors is often limited by the atmosphere: small particles in the atmosphere absorb and scatter the image-forming light from the object, so that the object's brightness approaches that of the background.[2] The greater the viewing distance, or the mistier the atmosphere, the greater the difference between the 'inherent contrast' (contrast at zero distance) and the 'effective contrast'[3] (contrast from the viewing distance). When the effective contrast is reduced to about 2 per cent, objects become invisible.

The reduction of contrast by the atmosphere can be used as a cue to distance, known as 'aerial perspective'. Surprisingly little quantitative work has been done on the use of this cue, though the general principle has been common knowledge for centuries, and the mathematical specification is now very precise. Brightness contrast drops off exponentially (rapidly at first and then more slowly), the rate depending upon the *attenuation coefficient* of the atmosphere.[4] The situation is similar under water, except that the attenuation coefficient is usually much larger: clear water, with a visibility of about 30 m, is equivalent to thick fog on land (Plate 1). Aerial perspective is a much more important cue under water than on land – partly because the loss of contrast is more noticeable, and partly because other distance cues are reduced or absent. Stereoscopic acuity, for example, is seriously impaired.[5] It is not surprising, then, that distances often appear exaggerated under water: over-estimation occurs at far distances in clear water,[6] and at distances beyond arm's length in murky water.[7] The over-estimation also increases with the turbidity of the water,[8] and distance judgements increase linearly as the logarithm of the brightness contrast decreases.[9] The latter function follows the physical change of contrast with distance, and suggests that aerial perspective is used as a systematic cue to distance.

Few experiments seem to have been conducted in air; but one outdoor experiment in a fog (visibility 30–130 m) showed that targets appeared to be about twice as far as in clear weather, and enlarged in size.[6] Fry and his colleagues[10] performed a laboratory simulation of aerial perspective by altering the brightness of the target against a constant background, in a clear atmosphere. The subjects made stereoscopic judgements of distance, which again varied linearly with the logarithm of the brightness contrast.

Despite a shortage of outdoor experiments, there is plenty of anecdotal evidence that distances seem diminished in the clear atmosphere of the desert, and exaggerated in a mist. However, there are some contradictory examples concerning bright lights at night, or patches of snow illuminated by moonlight. Usually these appear near. For example, Mauri and Bonatti were trying to keep awake on a dangerous ridge on the north face of the Laveredo, when Mauri experienced a visual illusion: 'There was one moment when the snowfield below us, lit up by the moonlight, seemed as if it had risen to where we were and that all I had to do was to stretch out a leg to reach it and at last be able to go to sleep.'[11] Murray reported a similar effect in Glencoe, when viewing the surrounding mountains in moonlight from the top of Buachaille Etive Mòr, over a cloudbank: '. . . this blanketing of intervening country, combined with the dazzle of their frozen snows, drew all the peaks unnaturally close in a fantastic optical illusion. Nevis looked but a stone's throw, and Bidean nam Bian a practicable leap.'[12] However, Bonington and Burke experienced the opposite effect on the Eiger: it was getting dark, and they could see a snowfield below them where they hoped to dig a snowhole for the night; they expected it to be about 70 m below them, but on abseiling down they found it was only 13 m.[13] It is also claimed that ships sometimes crash into rocks at night because the lighthouse appears further away than it really is.[14]

Lights glowing in the dark may well be a special case: there is nothing to compare with them, and they may appear either near or far. High-contrast objects may appear near only when other objects of different contrasts are present for comparison.

The contrast of outdoor objects is often hard to quantify because they have a split background. Objects on the horizon, for example, may border partly on a bright sky background and partly on a dark foreground. In such cases it seems likely that we pay more attention to the border of higher contrast: snow-capped mountains can be seen to stand out as nearer than the dark foothills, even though the peaks have little contrast with the white sky. Of course, other factors may contribute to this effect, such as the larger size of some main peaks in comparison with the foothills.[15]

II *Aerial Perspective and Colour Contrast*

Everyone knows that objects tend to become bluer in the distance, as well as fainter, because of the intervening atmosphere. It is also quite well known that there are 'advancing' and 'retreating' colours, reds normally appearing nearer than blues. This is possibly due to the learning of atmospheric cues: but the experimental literature is far from clear. Authors quote contradictory results, and few of them control or measure the luminosity and wavelength of the test objects.

A large part of the supposed colour effect is probably due to contrast, those colours which have the greater brightness or colour contrast with their background appearing nearer.[16] When the luminosity is equal, reds generally appear nearer than blues.[17] The effect is usually reversed in dim light, probably because blues appear brighter, the dark-adapted eye being more sensitive to blue than to red light. In daylight the eye is more sensitive to red. It is thus possible that apparent brightness, rather than colour-perspective cues, accounts for the apparent nearness of certain colours.[18]

It has so far been assumed that objects always become bluer in the distance. This is generally the case in a clear atmosphere or in clear water; but in a mist they become whiter, in peat lochs redder, and in green seas greener. Objects usually take on the colour of the intervening atmosphere or water – a colour which is partly determined by the size of the particles in the medium.

The sun gives out light of all wavelengths, which should mix to give an appearance of white light. However, a clear sky appears blue, because minute particles in the atmosphere scatter the blue light and absorb the red. A mist appears white, because the larger particles do not have such a selective effect, and scatter the different wavelengths more equally. Clear water appears blue for the same reason as the sky. If yellow substances are added to the water, as often happens round the coast, the blue end of the spectrum is absorbed, leaving green as the predominant colour. If the yellow substances are strong, as in peat lochs, more of the short wavelengths are absorbed, leaving a predominantly reddish-brown colour. The colour of the water becomes more monochromatic with depth. In clear water the red end of the spectrum is increasingly absorbed, leaving mainly blue light. In peat lochs, both the red light and the blue light are absorbed, leaving almost no light at all a few metres below the surface.

Objects appear coloured because they reflect some wavelengths and absorb others. It is the reflected light, in relation to that reflected by other objects, that largely determines the apparent colour. A coloured object cannot reflect wavelengths which are not present in the water; so if the relevant wavelengths are absent, it will appear black. That is why red objects appear black at some depth in a blue sea, and blue objects appear black at shallow depths in peat-stained water. Fluorescent colours do not obey these rules: they have the ability to absorb short wavelengths and convert them into longer wavelengths. Fluorescent reds can thus be seen at a depth where natural reds appear black. Such colours are brighter and more visible than natural colours in almost all circumstances.

The colours that divers claim to see under water are often nearer their 'true' colours than might be supposed from the preceding account. This is due to the fact that colour is always perceived in relation to the colours of surrounding objects: relative wavelength, rather than absolute wavelength, is what matters. Moreover, the eye adapts after a few minutes of exposure to a predominant wavelength, so that the sensitivity to small amounts of light of a contrasting wavelength is enhanced. When a diver first opens his eyes at moderate depth in a blue sea, red objects appear a muddy brown: but after a minute or two the red apparently deepens. This sensitisation to red makes the white light of an underwater torch appear tinged with red when first switched on at depth. It is not clear whether colour adaptation ceases after the first minute or so (as laboratory experiments suggest),[19] or whether it continues at a slow rate throughout a diving session. Subjectively, the blue or green cast of the sea eventually disappears; but no underwater experiments seem to have been done. Laboratory experiments are hardly a fair comparison: they lack the 'natural' quality of the underwater scene, where the dominant colour fills the visual field in all directions, and there are plenty of objects of known colour.

If the coloured light is strongly directional, and illuminates only part of the visual field, objects in its path appear coloured. This is because they are seen in contrast to objects which are illuminated by 'normal' or 'white' light. Thus the hills appear bathed in red when they are caught by the rays of the setting sun, either directly or by reflection from clouds. The redness of the sun is, of course, due to the scattering of the blue light by the atmosphere, only the redder rays being left to form an image: this effect is enhanced at sunrise and sunset, because the sun's rays pass through more of the earth's atmosphere than at noon.

Colour-contrast accounts for many of the surprising colours that can be seen on earth. For example, shadows on the white snow appear very blue in contrast to the yellow light of the sun, but turn to green during a pink sunset.

III *Brocken Spectres and Size-constancy*

The Brocken is the highest of the Harz mountains in Germany, and an excellent place for observing what has come to be known as the 'Brocken spectre'. One of the best accounts of the phenomenon was given by M. Haue in 1797. Haue was standing on the summit early one morning, with his back to the rising sun, when he saw a huge figure mimicking his actions, apparently at a great distance in the clouds ahead of him.[20] The same phenomenon is quite common in Scotland: it was described by James Hogg,[21] and probably lies behind the stories of the Grey Man of Ben MacDhui.[22]

The huge size of the shadow is sometimes said to be due to the great distance of the cloud or mist, the sun acting as a slide projector and the cloud as a screen. This is not entirely correct, because the sun's rays are virtually parallel and cast a shadow the same size as the object regardless of the distance of the 'screen' – provided the surface is perpendicular to the sun's rays. However, if the surface is tilted, the length of the shadow increases; and this situation arises when a low sun casts a shadow onto a cloudbank below (Plate 2).

The optical distance of the Brocken spectre is normally quite close,[23] and the enlargement is due more to perceptual than physical factors. The explanation is the same as for other objects seen in a mist – aerial perspective makes them look more distant than they are, and the apparent size increases roughly in proportion to the apparent distance.

At first sight, this explanation may seem wrong, since real objects become optically *smaller* in the distance, not larger (Fig. 3.1a). However, the brain enlarges distant objects so as to compensate for the decrease in retinal image size: the result is

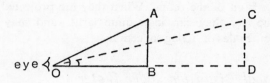

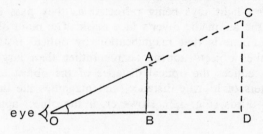

FIGURE 3.1

Two aspects of 'size-constancy'. (a) Normally the object is of constant size (AB = CD), but the angular size of the image subtended at the eye decreases with the viewing distance (CÔD < AÔB). The brain makes some allowance for the latter effect, so that the apparent size of an object changes much less than might be predicted from the image size. (b) In some cases (such as after-images, or misperceptions of distance) the angular size remains constant (AÔB = CÔD), because the change in apparent viewing distance does not correspond to a change in the location of a real object. The brain nevertheless compensates as for (a), with the result that CD appears larger than AB.

that the apparent decrease in size is much less than might be expected from the smaller image. This compensatory system is known as 'size-constancy'. When there is a discrepancy between the true distance and the apparent distance, the apparent size is correspondingly distorted (Fig. 3.1b).

The compensatory system is very obvious with 'after-images'. After-images are the images that persist after staring at a bright light: they have no real distance or location, existing only as stimulation from the retina. They can be 'projected' onto different surfaces, and their apparent size grows with the apparent distance. The same applies to other images arising within the eye, such as those due to the specks and air bubbles floating in the fluid in front of the retina. When they are projected onto a distant blue sky they can look quite large – and may be the origin of some tales of 'flying saucers'.

IV   *Optical Distortion under Water*

It is well known that objects appear enlarged under water, but the reason for this is less familiar.[24] Magnification is often given as the cause, light rays being refracted as they pass between water and the air in the diver's face mask. The main objection to this argument is that magnification by optical instruments usually makes objects appear nearer rather than larger. The face mask reduces the optical distance of the object to about three quarters of its true distance, and magnifies the image by about four thirds (Fig. 3.2). However, if the object appears to

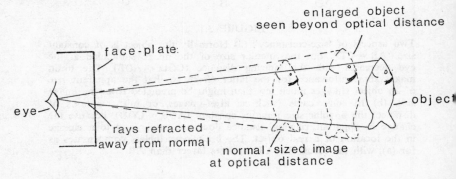

enlarged object
seen beyond optical distance

face-plate

eye

rays refracted
away from normal

normal-sized image
at optical distance

object

FIGURE 3.2

An object viewed through a face-mask under water is magnified and reduced in distance by refraction, but its apparent size varies with its apparent distance.

be at its optical distance, there is no good reason why it should appear enlarged: if a real object is placed at three quarters of its previous distance, its retinal image size is also enlarged by about four thirds, but it does not appear magnified. So what is the difference under water?

There is probably more than one reason for the difference.

One factor is that the exaggerated aerial perspective makes objects appear further away than the optical distance, and the brain enlarges them as if they were at the far distance. This explanation accounts quite well for the apparent size of distant objects;[6] but not for very close objects in clear water, which are usually judged to be near the optical distance.[25] Objects within arm's reach – even familiar objects such as one's own hand – may appear too large. The probable explanation is that a conflict arises between vision and touch – the hand looks too near, but is felt to be at its proper distance; alternatively, it appears to be at its proper distance, but looks larger than it feels.

The poor diver finds himself in an impossible situation: he cannot get both the size and the distance right at the same time, and usually he gets both wrong. There is one solution – to change the rules about the relationship between size and distance, so that both can be perceived correctly. Divers find it very difficult to do this, as it means reversing the habit of a life-time. (It may even be more than a habit, since some degree of size-constancy is present in very young infants.)[26] Divers respond to the conflict in different ways, some perceiving mainly size-distortion, and others mainly distance-distortion. If the diver moves around under water, or handles objects, he begins to adapt to some aspect of the distortion. Some divers adapt to size and *counter-adapt* (perceive increased distortion) to distance; others do the opposite; and a few manage to adapt both to size and to distance, thus learning new size-constancy rules which are appropriate to the underwater situation.[27]

Refraction at the face-mask introduces other distortions beside those of size and distance. Straight lines appear curved, giving an effect known as 'pincushion distortion'. The apparent direction of objects is also distorted when they are viewed obliquely: points on the left of the face-mask are displaced to the left, and those on the right to the right, the degree of displacement increasing in the periphery. Divers adapt quite well to the curvature distortion,[28] but have some difficulty with the lateral displacements.[29] They can adapt easily to unidirectional distortion, but make little headway with two opposing distortions.

Many experimenters measure perceptual distortion and adaptation by changes in 'eye-hand co-ordination' – changes in the accuracy of reaching for targets without continuous visual guidance.[29-31] Indeed, some would argue that adaptation is due to a change in the felt position of the hand, or to a change in the relation between vision and touch, rather than to a change in how things look. Adaptation probably occurs in any or all of these systems, depending upon the experimental circumstances. A diver is normally free to swim around, touch familiar objects, and learn about refraction from lectures and books: he can therefore adapt in all possible ways.

A theoretical issue of more relevance to divers is that of 'conditioned adaptation'. A diver does not completely 'forget' the adaptation that occurs during the course of a dive: at the start of each subsequent dive the underwater world appears a little more normal, and adaptation proceeds a little more rapidly. A perfectly adapted amphibious person would presumably 'switch on' to underwater vision immediately he submerged, and would 'switch back' to air vision immediately he emerged: he would suffer no underwater distortion and no after-effect in the air. It is doubtful whether any divers spend sufficient time under water to reach that state. Given enough practice they might achieve it, just as people do who regularly take their glasses off and on. (Lenses which correct for short sight, or other defects, often cause changes in apparent size or distance; but these changes are soon ignored.) It is not entirely clear how such 'conditioned' or 'situational' adaptation occurs. It seems likely that some degree of adaptation becomes conditioned to the wearing of the face mask or goggles,[32] and some to other aspects of the underwater situation; and some is probably explained by a very quick reaction to the optical deformation that occurs as the head is moved around.[24]

There are many other optical distortions which people are likely to meet in normal life. Spectacles, thick glass windows, and concave wing mirrors on cars, are common examples. These differ from the distortions investigated by early psychologists in being far less extreme. For example, in the 1890s Stratton[33] investigated the effects of inverting the retinal image – a very difficult distortion to cope with. Natural distortions also differ in that they occur intermittently, while early experimenters usually wore goggles continuously for days on end. Modern laboratory experiments are normally short, but are perhaps even further removed from everyday life: the subject typically sits at a table with his head clamped in one position, wearing wedge prisms which shift everything a few degrees to one side, and is tested for his ability to point at lights glowing in the dark. Neither the type of optical distortion, nor the conditions of training and testing, bear much relation to natural situations.

V Carpentered Environments

It is clear that one's normal visual environment affects the way one perceives other environments. This is evident from the previous examples of aerial perspective and optical distortions; and it is also true of other kinds of environmental difference, such as the difference between dense forest and open country. The latter point is well illustrated by an observation of Turnbull in Africa: he took a young Pygmy man from the Ituri forest in the Congo for a drive in the open, and the man was unable to appreciate the size or distance of cattle; he thought they were insects which grew in size as he approached them. He had never been able to see beyond a few yards in the dense forest, or perhaps a quarter of a mile on roads near the forest, and could not interpret the distance cues in open country.[34]

Other attempts to show differences in spatial perception between people of different visual backgrounds (or 'ecological environments') have not been so successful. Much work has centered round the idea that geometrical illusions are due to the inappropriate interpretation of learned perspective cues; and that cultural differences in susceptibility to such illusions are due to different experiences with perspective cues in the native environment.[35] For example, a 'carpentered' or 'urban' environment is supposed to make the inhabitants familiar with linear perspective; they should thus be especially susceptible to the Müller-Lyer illusion, which is said to be due to a perspective interpretation of acute or obtuse angles. Conversely, a flat and open environment is supposed to familiarise the inhabitants with foreshortened views of roads receding into the distance; they learn to compensate for this by expanding lines which form a vertical image on the retina, and are thus especially susceptible

Müller-Lyer Illusion

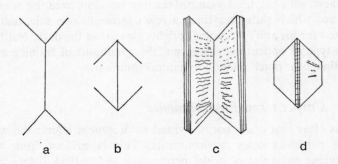

a   b   c   d

Horizontal-Vertical Illusion

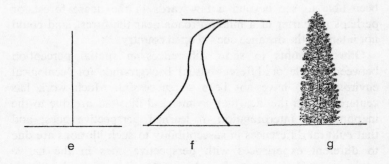

e   f   g

FIGURE 3.3

In the Müller-Lyer illusion, the vertical line in (a) appears longer than
in (b), though both are equal. According to the perspective theory, the
former typically represents a more distant view than the latter – such as
the inside view of the spine of a book (c), rather than the outside view
(d). In the Horizontal-Vertical illusion, the vertical line in (e) appears
longer than the horizontal line. It is said to represent the foreshortened
view of a flat road (f), rather than the unforeshortened view of an
upright tree (g). The illusions are said to occur because the brain
expands the typically-more-distant lines.

to the horizontal-vertical illusion (Fig. 3.3). Cross-cultural studies of the geometrical illusions were first carried out by Rivers around 1900, during the Cambridge Anthropological Expedition to the Torres Straits,[36] and a later expedition to investigate the Todas of South India.[37] Since then many authors have confirmed the general tendency for Europeans to be more susceptible to the Müller-Lyer and less susceptible to the horizontal-vertical illusion than non-Europeans. Unfortunately for the theory, there is little evidence to show that such differences are due to variations in the 'carpenteredness' of the environment. There are other cultural differences (such as education), and racial differences (such as retinal pigmentation), which may contribute to the illusions.[38] Carefully controlled studies in Ghana and Australia failed to show the predicted relationship between visual environment and illusion-susceptibility. Regardless of the question of cultural or racial differences, there are many other reasons for doubting the perspective theory of the illusions.[39] A minor objection, which is sometimes raised, is that the illusions occur for three-dimensional objects viewed in natural settings out of doors;[40] yet they are supposed to be due to the inappropriate but compelling nature of the perspective cues when drawn on paper. It is argued that the true perspective of real objects should be sufficiently unambiguous to remove all distortion. However, the brain tends to compromise when faced with conflicting spatial cues; and it is, perhaps, no more surprising that the geometrical illusions should work for solid objects than on paper.

It has also been suggested that there are cultural, racial or environmental differences in the ability to interpret photographs and drawings; in laboratory tests of size-constancy; in the perception of the vertical when the visual framework is tilted; and in many other perceptual abilities.[41] If such differences exist, they probably have more to do with education than with carpentered environments.

VI *Off-sized Environments*

There is a place in Perthshire called the 'The Sma' Glen'. It is a favourite spot for tourists, because the mountains look most impressive despite the fact that everything is on a miniature scale. The highest mountains are not more than 500 m above road level; yet the effect is not much smaller than Glencoe, where the mountains rise to 1,000 m above the road. Part of this effect is due to the fact that the summits of high mountains are rarely seen from the road, being obscured by lower 'false summits'. Nevertheless, the visible height of the Glencoe mountains is considerably larger than the Sma' Glen mountains. The probable explanation is that apparent size is greatly influenced by the relative sizes of other objects in the field of view; and there are no other larger mountains nearby which can have a dwarfing effect on the Sma' Glen.

'Familiar size' can also affect spatial perception. When other size and distance cues are weak, there is a tendency to see a familiar object as though it were at an appropriate distance for its retinal size. Thus a miniature object may be seen as normal in size but too distant, and an enlarged version may seem normal but too near. Usually, however, there is a compromise, with the object appearing both off-sized and at the wrong distance.[42] Some very large objects, such as power stations and radio telescopes, can be considered as off-sized: we expect them to be smaller than they are, and unless they are seen in relation to familiar objects their size and distance is hard to gauge. A particularly difficult case is the Fylingdales early-warning station: three mysterious white globes lie, like ping-pong balls, across the heather of the North Yorkshire moors (Plate 3). A party of walkers, whom I was with, assumed from a distance that the globes were about the size of a house – but on approaching we realised that they were four or five times that size.

Neither familiar size, nor relative size, nor compensation for apparent distance, is sufficiently effective to produce perfect size-constancy at all distances. Objects undoubtedly appear somewhat smaller in the distance, even though they are recognised intellectually as 'normal size'. This change in apparent size of familiar objects can be used as a cue to distance. Parachutists, for example, can judge when to open the parachute (at about 700 m) from the apparent size of the hangars, the width of the road, and other cues. This sort of judgement can, of course, go badly wrong in off-sized environments. For example, Smith reported looking down from a balloon on to the Ngorongoro

Crater, and being unable to see the animals at first because they were so much smaller than he had expected: the crater is huge, twelve miles across, and lacking in obvious size cues.[43] Similarly, astronauts have complained that it is impossible to tell the distance of mountains on the moon: they might be any size or distance, and there is no aerial perspective to help matters.

Recognition of familiar size must in some way depend on the size of one's own body. Most people have had the experience of revisiting childhood scenes, and discovering that the places and people are very much smaller than they had remembered. Presumably one updates one's ideas about the proper size of objects as one's body grows.

VII *Looking Up and Down*

Everyone is agreed that objects tend to look too small when viewed from a great height, or from below. Cars in the street look tiny from a high building; and swimmers on the surface of the water may appear minute to a diver deep below.[9] There is much less agreement about apparent distance. Some, like Baden-Powell,[1] would claim that distance is underestimated, while others maintain the opposite. Dennis Gray, for example, describes falling off a rock ledge and spinning upside down on the end of a rope: '. . . the rock face seemed to be revolving and the walls of the rock to be expanding, and from my upside down position the ground seemed hundreds of feet away instead of the eighty or so it really was. I had lost all perspective . . .'[44] This may, of course, be a case of fear expanding the apparent distance; but there are several innocuous laboratory experiments on vertical viewing which show both over-estimation and under-estimation.

There are two main classes of theory to explain the effects: visual, and proprioceptive. Visual theories maintain that the size or distance cues are different when looking vertically than when looking horizontally. Space is relatively empty when looking up or down, whereas it is normally filled with objects when looking horizontally: filled space makes things look further away, and therefore enlarged; while unfilled space makes them look near and small. According to this argument, conflicting reports about apparent distance are due to people using altered apparent size as an intellectual or 'second level' cue to distance: objects basically look small and near when viewed vertically, but their smallness also gives a paradoxical impression of great distance. A different visual theory is that the size cues, rather than the distance cues, are changed: objects viewed horizontally seem quite large relative to other small objects, whereas objects viewed vertically are seen in isolation or in relation to large spaces. This may be true for the upward viewing of isolated objects in the air, such as planes, but it is not usually true of downward viewing. There are, of course, some trick cases where the size cues are misleading, such as looking down a scree slope: in this case the rocks are larger at the bottom than the top, the laws of gravity opposing the laws of perspective.

Visual cues undoubtedly account for part of the difference between horizontal and vertical viewing; but perceptual differences remain even when the visual scene is the same in all directions – a situation which can be contrived by the use of mirrors or models. Moreover, a horizontal scene looks distinctly odd if one looks through one's legs, or lies down: objects again look too small, and either too far or too near. For these reasons, 'proprioceptive' theories have been advanced: size and distance perception are said to be learned during normal horizontal viewing, and any change in the orientation of the body is sufficient to disturb perception. Such activities as raising the eyes, tilting the head, or inverting the body, interfere with normal spatial perception and size-constancy.

This version of the proprioceptive theory is imprecise. The trouble is not that people are unused to looking up or down, but that when they do so the objects they see are normally much closer than objects viewed horizontally. Objects at one's feet or near one's head are nearer than objects at the horizon – so it is entirely reasonable to reduce the apparent size and distance indicated by the retinal image, in relation to that indicated for horizontal objects.

Visual and proprioceptive theories can be combined, if it is accepted that man's perceptual system is acting in a manner that is *normally* appropriate for vertical viewing. Any cue that suggests vertical viewing, whether visual or proprioceptive, is sufficient to trigger the 'reduced-size' response. This response becomes inappropriate when looking down from great heights, or looking up at very high objects, or when looking at a normal horizontal scene in an unusual bodily position. However, given practice at such activities, people learn to scale size and distances more appropriately: the street view from a tall building soon appears normal,[45] and divers quickly learn to estimate the correct distance to the surface of the water.[46]

VIII   *The Celestial Dome and the Moon Illusion*

Perhaps the most famous of outdoor illusions is the 'moon illusion': the moon (and other celestial bodies) look larger on the horizon than in the zenith. Size changes in individual stars are not obvious; but the effect can be seen in those constellations (such as Pegasus and Orion) which rise and set low on the horizon, but reach a moderate height when due south.

Explanations of the illusion are manifold,[39] but fall into the same categories as those just described for vertical viewing. One of the most popular visual theories is that the illusion is due to the 'flattened dome' of the sky: the zenith appears nearer than the horizon (because it is empty), thus flattening the truly-spherical heavens; and the reduced apparent distance of the zenith moon leads to a reduced apparent size (Fig. 3.4).

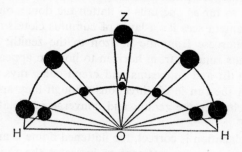

FIGURE 3.4

Flattened-dome theory of the moon illusion. The observer at O sees the celestial hemisphere (HZH) as a flattened dome (HAH), the apparent height of the zenith being reduced from Z to A. The angular size of the moon remains the same at all elevations, but the apparent size shrinks with the apparent distance. (After E. G. Boring, 'The moon illusion', *Amer. J. Physics*, 1943, Vol. 11, pp. 55–60.)

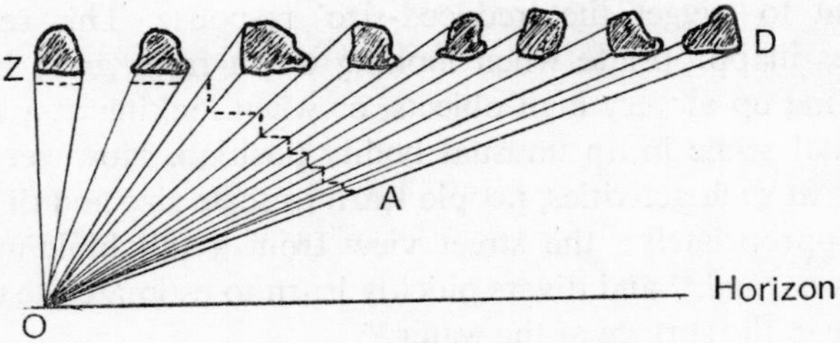

FIGURE 3.5

Perspective view of the clouds. An observer at O sees a horizontal layer of clouds (ZD) as a stair-step pattern (ZA), the further clouds appearing as near as the zenith clouds. (After W. J. Humphreys, *Physics of the Air*, New York: Dover, 1964, p. 451.)

People disagree about the apparent distance of the moon, but most would agree that the empty sky appears as a flattened dome. This flattening of the dome is usually regarded by psychologists as a perceptual error, with no useful function. This view is probably incorrect: as argued in the previous section, vertical distances normally *are* nearer than horizontal distances. Clear skies are a fairly rare sight, at least in Britain; a more typical situation is a cloud bank, the lower clouds being at a uniform height above the ground (Fig. 3.5). In this case the clouds on the horizon really are further away than those at the zenith, and the perceptual flattening of the dome is an adaptive response. In so far as one fails to flatten the dome, one sees the sky as the camera sees it: a layer of cumulus clouds appears to rise like a staircase from the horizon to the zenith; a straight band of clouds running from horizon to horizon appears to arch over the zenith; and sunbeams and crepuscular rays appear to diverge from the sun in all directions (though they are virtually parallel), arch over the zenith, and converge again at the anti-solar point.[47]

If this explanation is correct, the flattened dome is an adaptive perceptual response – an attempt to interpret the retinal image of the objects in the sky correctly. This response produces illusions in the case of celestial bodies, because (unlike clouds and aeroplanes), their distance remains constant in all directions.

IX *The Terrestrial Saucer and the Subjective Horizon*

The converse effect of the arching clouds is the concave earth, as seen from a balloon or plane (Fig. 3.6). If one is flying between two layers of clouds, one seems to be between two enormous watch glasses, concave both up and down.[48] Again, the downward view seems to be due to a compromise between the 'spherical' retinal image (all points being considered equidistant), and the true state of affairs in which points on the horizon are further away.

We are well practised at interpreting the retinal image, or photograph, of a ground-level view to the horizon. We realize that the points higher up the picture are further away, and not necessarily higher, than those in the foreground at the bottom of the picture. We are not so good at interpreting the view from a height, and tend to perceive objects on the horizon as high rather than far. This effect can often be seen when looking at the sea from a high mountain: the sea appears to be much higher than it should be, and one gets the impression that it might overflow into the valley below. The sea also appears to slope, and if the outline of the sea is broken by hills it is hard to believe that the different sections are on the same level:

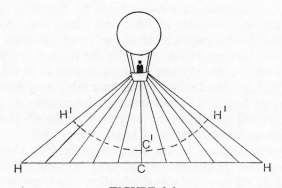

FIGURE 3.6

The 'terrestrial saucer' or 'concave earth'. Failure to appreciate that H is further away than C makes the flat surface HCH become the curved surface H¹ C¹ H¹.

they look like separate lochs rather than unbroken sea (Plate 4).

There are, of course, refractive effects due to the changing temperature of the atmosphere which can affect the optical distance and level of the horizon, causing 'looming', 'towering' and mirages. This is particularly likely to happen at sea, where the temperature changes are sharp. It may also occur with an increase in height, as the temperature normally drops by about 5°C every kilometre. This has the effect of raising the optical height of distant objects, and consequently extending the distance to the horizon beyond what might be expected geometrically.[47] However, the optical refraction is normally much too small to account for the apparent raising of the horizon when viewed from a height. This effect must be due to a failure to interpret the unusual perspective, or to some other psychological factors.

A similar effect to the raised horizon is the raised apparent height of surrounding mountains. Peaks which are level with one's own summit appear considerably higher, and all points on the opposite mountains are raised correspondingly. Cornish[49] estimated the error to be $6\frac{1}{2}°$ as measured from sketches of mountain scenes. My memory estimate is also about 6°: Stob Binnean and Ben More (Perthshire) appear to be about 200 m higher than each other, when both are about 1,170 m, and 2 km apart.

Many explanations have been offered for the raised height of mountains. MacDougall[50] in 1903, and others since, have suggested that the descending slope of one's own mountain is taken to be more horizontal than it is, with the result that truly horizontal points on the opposite mountain appear to be above eye-level (Fig. 3.7a). MacDougall found from laboratory experiments that sloping lines can indeed influence judgements of eye-level in the expected way. However this cannot be the whole explanation, because over-estimation of height occurs when the slope of one's own mountain is hidden in a precipitous drop. Others have suggested that judgement of eye-level is normally too low, resulting in the over-estimation of points which are actually at eye-level (Fig. 3.7b); however, only adult males are supposed to show this error, while women and children err in the opposite direction.[51] It is not clear that laboratory experiments on eye-level have much to do with the apparent height of mountains: there is no evidence of any sex difference in the latter type of judgement.

Minnaert[48] suggests that mountain heights are over-estimated because they are projected onto the celestial dome, the lower part of which is expanded. This belongs to a more plausible class of explanation, though it appears to be the wrong way round. The expansion of the lower part of the dome is due to the attempt to enlarge objects on the horizon to their 'correct'

(a) Mistaken–slope theory

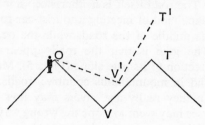

(b) Mistaken-eye-level theory

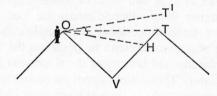

FIGURE 3.7

Two attempts to explain the apparent raising of the height of mountains when viewed across a valley. (a) The slope OV appears flatter than reality (OV¹), with consequent steepening and raising of the opposite slope from VT to V¹T¹. (b) Estimates of eye-level are mistaken, the apparent horizontal being too low (OH rather than OT). The apparent level of T is thus raised to T¹, the angle of elevation (TÔT¹) being equal to the angle of error of the horizontal (HÔT).

size – it cannot be used to explain any supposed *over-correction*. In fact, *under-correction* is the normal rule; but, when viewing from a height, this causes an apparent elevation of the horizon and other low-level objects (Fig. 3.6). This 'terrestrial saucer' explanation can also account for the raising of objects at eye-level, if it is assumed that they appear raised in relation to the elevated low-level foreground.

X *Slope Perception and the Electric Brae*

The 'Electric Brae' is a dangerous stretch of road in hilly country near Ayr.[52] The road itself is neither steep nor 'live': the danger lies in the likelihood of meeting a tourist-car rolling slowly backwards in the middle of the road, while the occupants roar with laughter. The joke is that the road appears to slope in the opposite direction to its true slope (Plate 5). Many similar places can be found in mountainous country: roads appear flatter or steeper than they really are, rivers may flow uphill, and parts of golf courses may seem to slope the wrong way.[53]

Slope illusions can occur because of the misperception of bodily orientation (Ch. 5). However, the mountain road illusions are generally visible in films and photographs, so they must be mainly visual in origin. The difficulty seems to be that there are few cues which unambiguously indicate frontal slope, and the observer is easily misled by surrounding slopes or other irrelevant contextual cues.

There are at least two sorts of visual cues the viewer might use in judging slope: three-dimensional and two-dimensional. The use of three-dimensional cues implies that the viewer is something of a geometrician: he perceives the true distance and height of the top and bottom of the slope, and thus perceives its true inclination. These cues cannot be adequately represented in a frontal photograph or sketch, since they include head movements and binocular vision. Using three-dimensional cues, any error in height or distance judgements should cause a corresponding error in slope judgements.[54] Profile views of some of these errors are shown in Fig. 3.8.

Slope can also be judged directly from the two-dimensional perspective cues visible in a frontal sketch or photograph (Fig.

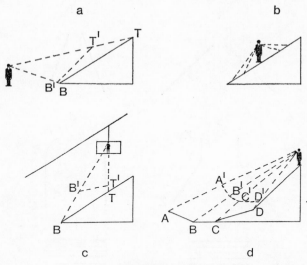

FIGURE 3.8

Three-dimensional aspects of slope illusions. (a) The uphill view of a slope (BT) looks steeper (B^1T^1) from afar, because the distance to the top is foreshortened. (b) When standing on a slope there is less foreshortening, and both uphill and downhill views should be fairly realistic. (c) When viewed from a height (as from a cable-car or chair-lift), the downhill view (BT) is flattened (B^1T^1) due to the foreshortening of the distance to the bottom. (d) When looking down to a valley, the downhill slope appears flattened, the flat valley rises up, and the opposite slope rises steeply (ABCD becomes $A^1B^1C^1D^1$). Both (c) and (d) are examples of the 'terrestrial saucer' effect.

3.9). These include such factors as the degree of convergence of 'vertical' lines, and the rate of change of spacing of 'horizontal' lines – the former probably being the more important cue.[55] These cues are ambiguous, because they vary with the viewing distance in addition to the slope: strong convergence can mean that the eye or camera is very close to the slope, or that the slope is fairly flat. Any change in convergence certainly indicates a change in the degree or direction of slope; but the absolute angle of slope is not given.

To give meaning to the perspective cues, one has to know what the picture represents: trees, fenceposts, mountains and the sky usually make it unambiguous. The most critical portion of

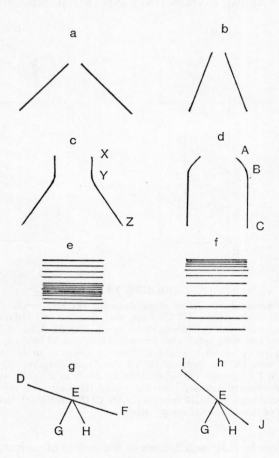

FIGURE 3.9

Two-dimensional slope cues. Degree of convergence is important, (a) appearing flatter than (b) – but (a) could be a closer view of the same slope as (b). In (c) there is a change of convergence at Y; but XY could be uphill in relation to a flat YZ, or flat in relation to a downhill YZ, or overhanging in relation to an uphill YZ. Similarly in (d) there is a convergence change at B, with AB being flatter, downhill or underhanging in relation to BC. The horizontal spacing gradients corresponding to the linear perspectives of (c) and (d) are shown in (e) and (f). Additional sloping lines affect the interpretation: the frontal surface GEH appears steeper in (h) than (g), perhaps because it is assimilated to the steep profile line IEJ rather than the flatter line DEF.

the picture is the change of contour where a downhill road meets a flat valley, or a flat road meets a mountain, or an uphill road meets the sky. This is probably the main cause of error at the Electric Brae: the truly downhill view meets a sky background, while the truly uphill view runs into a wooded valley and a mountain background. Doubtless other sloping lines in the field of view contribute to the effect, but the background is obviously important.

Even when no illusory features are present, there is a strong tendency to over-estimate the steepness of a frontal slope. The over-estimation increases at night, and when viewing from a distance – conditions in which three-dimensional cues are much reduced. However, climbers and skiers frequently over-estimate slopes in broad daylight, when in contact with the slope. Murray[12] noticed this effect when climbing: he measured the angle of the pitch with a clinometer, and found that an estimated 68° was actually 63°, and an estimated 'vertical' was only 77°. I found similar results for skiers: thirty skiers standing on a 24° slope gave a mean judgement of 37°. A different group of thirty-seven skiers, judging a similar angle of slope from some distance below, gave a mean estimate of 47°. The increased error of this group was probably due both to more distant viewing, and to the fact that it contained less experienced skiers. Experienced skiers or mountaineers gave more accurate judgements than novices, and men than women. Experience may lead to factual knowledge – such as that snow does not lie well on slopes over 50°, and that most ski slopes are considerably less than 40°. Experience also lessens fear, and thus reduces the tendency for a climber to say 'vertical' when he means 'too steep to climb'. Most mountaineers and skiers would also admit that experience produces a genuine perceptual change: slopes really do look less steep once one has conquered them.

It is sometimes claimed that slopes look steeper, or flatter, when viewed downhill rather than uphill; but there seems to be no evidence to support either difference. I found the judgements of skiers standing on a slope were approximately the same in both viewing directions. Kammann, in a city experiment, also found the usual over-estimates for downhill viewing – a 34° hill was estimated at 48° by men and 55° by women; and 20°

street slopes were estimated from memory at 38° (presumably from a mixture of uphill and downhill memories).[54] Any directional differences are probably small, or are due to other factors. For example, downhill slopes are normally viewed whilst on the slope, whereas uphill views are often viewed from a considerable distance; and most people have very limited experience of steep downhill views, whereas they often see the corresponding uphill views.

In this chapter many examples have been given of visual cues which are 'ecologically valid' in one environment, but become 'invalid' in another – at least until the viewer learns to re-interpret them. The next chapter treats some auditory transformations in a similar manner, and considers some of the communication difficulties which arise in different environments.

NOTES

1   R. S. S. Baden-Powell, *Scouting for Boys*, London: C. Arthur Pearson, 1944, p. 70.

2   For a clear description of light and colour in the atmosphere and under water, see J. N. Lythgoe, 'Vision', Ch. 4 in *Underwater Science*, edited by J. D. Woods and J. N. Lythgoe, London: Oxford University Press, 1971.

3   The effective contrast is often described as the *apparent contrast* by physicists; but psychologists prefer to reserve the word 'apparent' for phenomena due to the brain and sense organs, rather than for physical phenomena. It is quite possible that the 'apparent contrast' as judged by an observer, is not the same as the 'effective contrast' as measured by a light meter.

4   The inherent contrast (C_o) of an object at zero distance is given by $C_o = \frac{O-B}{B}$ where O is the object brightness and B is the background brightness. The effective contrast (C_r) of the same object viewed from distance r is given by $C_r = C_o$ exp. $(-\alpha r)$, where α is the beam attenuation coefficient. This equation applies for horizontal sightings, both in air and under water. For further details and explanations, see J. N. Lythgoe (Ref. 2).

5   Stereoscopic acuity is the ability of the brain to perceive differences in distance, or perceive objects as 'solid', by noting the disparity between the images received by the two eyes. This ability is impaired under water for several reasons, of which low brightness-contrast and reduced peripheral vision are probably the most important. Further details can be found in the following papers: H. E. Ross, 'Stereoscopic acuity under water', *Underwater Ass. Rep.* 1966–67, Vol. 2, pp. 61–4; S. M. Luria, 'Stereoscopic acuity underwater', *Amer. J. Psychol.* 1968, Vol. 81, pp. 359–66; S. M. Luria and

J. A. S. Kinney, 'Peripheral stimuli and stereoacuity under water', *Percept. Psychophys.* 1972, Vol. 11, pp. 437–40.

6   H. E. Ross, 'Water, fog and the size-distance invariance hypothesis', *Brit. J. Psychol.*, 1967, Vol. 58, pp. 301–13.

7   P. R. Kent, 'Vision under water', *Amer. J. Optom. and A.M.A. Optom.*, 1966, Vol. 43, pp. 553–65; S. M. Luria, J. A. S. Kinney and S. Weissman, 'Estimates of size and distance underwater', *Amer. J. Psychol.*, 1967, Vol. 80, pp. 282–6.

8   J. A. S. Kinney, S. M. Luria and D. O. Weitzman, 'Effect of turbidity on judgements of distance underwater', *Percept. Mot. Skills*, 1969, Vol. 28, pp. 331–3.

9   H. E. Ross, 'Spatial perception under water', Ch. 3 in *Underwater Science*, edited by J. D. Woods and J. N. Lythgoe, London: Oxford University Press, 1971.

10 G. A. Fry, C. S. Bridgman and V. J. Ellerbrock, 'The effects of atmospheric scattering on binocular depth perception', *Amer. J. Optom.*, 1949, Vol. 26, pp. 9–15.

11 W. Bonatti, *On the Heights* (translated by L. F. Edwards), London: Hart-Davis, 1964, p. 55.

12 W. H. Murray, *Mountaineering in Scotland*, London: Dent, 1947, p. 225; pp. 40–1.

13 P. Gillman and D. Haston, *Eiger Direct*, London: Collins, 1966, p. 148.

14 W. J. Lewis, *Ceaseless Vigil*, London: Harrap, 1970, p. 34.

15 J. J. Gibson and H. Flock, 'The apparent distance of mountains', *Amer. J. Psychol.*, 1962, Vol. 75, pp. 501–3.

16 W. M. Smith, Unpublished experiment reported in *Visual Space Perception* by W. H. Ittelson, New York: Springer, 1960, p. 101.

17 R. Over, 'Stimulus wavelength variation and size and distance judgements', *Brit. J. Psychol.*, 1962, Vol. 53, pp. 141–7.

18 A further explanation, favoured by physicists, is the idea of 'Colour stereoscopy'. It was invented in 1885 by Einthoven, and is still current (W. Einthoven, 'Stereoscopic durch Farbendifferenz', *Graefes Arch. für Ophthal.*, 1885, Vol. 31, pp. 211–38; K. N. Ogle, 'Special topics in binocular spatial localization', Ch. 17 in *The Eye*, Vol. 4, edited by H. Davson, New York: Academic Press, 1962). The basic idea is that the binocular disparities of red and blue images are different, due to the chromatic aberration of the lens and the asymmetry of the fovea. Red is said to be stereoscopically nearer by day, and blue by night. However, colour stereopsis cannot be very important, since the colour-distance effects occur quite strongly with only one eye (R. Over, Ref. 17). Moreover, the effects depend upon perceived colour rather than wavelength; colour-blind people do not see them, though their lenses are subject to chromatic aberration like those of normal people (T. Oyama and T. Yamamura, 'The effect of hue and brightness on the depth perception in normal and color-blind subjects', *Psychologica*, 1960, Vol. 3, pp. 191–4.

19 J. A. S. Kinney and J. C. Cooper, 'Adaptation to a homochromatic visual world', Rep. No. 499, U.S. Naval Submarine Medical Center, Groton, Conn. 1967.

20 D. Brewster, *Letters on Natural Magic*, London: Murray, 1832, p. 129.

21 J. Hogg, *The Private Memoirs and Confessions of a Justified Sinner*, Oxford: Oxford University Press, 1970.

22 For some other explanations, see A. Grey, *The Big Grey Man of Ben MacDhui*, Aberdeen: Impulse Books, 1970.

23 T. Weir, 'Spectres of the hills', *Scottish Field*, January 1966, p. 32.

24 H. E. Ross, S. S. Franklin and P. Lennie, 'Adaptation of divers to size distortion under water', *Brit. J. Psychol.*, 1970, Vol. 61, pp. 365–73.

25 H. Ono, J. P. O'Reilly and L. M. Herman, 'Underwater distance distortion within the manual work space', *Human Factors*, 1970, Vol. 12, pp. 473–80.

26 T. G. R. Bower, 'The visual world of infants', *Scientific American*, 1966, Vol. 215, pp. 80–92.

27 S. S. Franklin, H. E. Ross and G. Weltman, 'Size-distance invariance in perceptual adaptation', *Psychon. Sci.*, 1970, Vol. 21, pp. 229–31.

28 H. E. Ross, 'Adaptation of divers to curvature distortion under water', *Ergonomics*, 1970, Vol. 13, pp. 489–99.

29 H. E. Ross and P. Lennie, 'Adaptation and counter-adaptation to complex optical distortion', *Perception and Psychophysics*, 1972, Vol. 12, pp. 273–77.

30 H. Ono and J. P. O'Reilly, 'Adaptation to underwater distance distortion as a function of different sensory-motor tasks', *Human Factors*, 1971, Vol. 13, pp. 133–40.

31 S. M. Luria and J. A. S. Kinney, 'Underwater vision', *Science*, 1970, Vol. 167, pp. 1454–61.

32 R. B. Welch, 'Discriminative conditioning of prism adaptation', *Perception and Psychophysics*, 1971, Vol. 10, pp. 90–2.

33 An excellent discussion of both Stratton's work and more recent approaches to optical distortion can be found in: W. Epstein, *Varieties of Perceptual Learning*, Ch. 9, New York: McGraw-Hill, 1967.

34 C. M. Turnbull, 'Some observations regarding the experiences and behaviour of the BaMbuti Pygmies', *Amer. J. Psychol.*, 1961, Vol. 74, pp. 304–8.

35 M. H. Segall, D. T. Campbell and M. J. Herskovits, *The Influence of Culture on Visual Perception*, Indianapolis: Bobbs-Merill, 1966.

36 W. H. R. Rivers, 'Vision', in *Reports of the Cambridge Anthropological Expedition to the Torres Straits*, Vol. 2, Part 1, edited by A. C. Haddon, Cambridge: Cambridge University Press, 1901.

37 W. H. R. Rivers, 'Observations on the senses of the Todas', *Brit. J. Psychol.*, 1905, Vol. 1, pp. 321–96.

38 G. Jahoda, 'Retinal pigmentation, illusion susceptibility and space perception', *Int. J. Psychol.*, 1971, Vol. 6, pp. 199–208.

39 For a review of cross-cultural studies, and theories of the illusions, see: J. O. Robinson, *The Psychology of Visual Illusion*, London: Hutchinson, 1972.

40 A. Chapanis and D. A. Mankin, 'The vertical-horizontal illusion in a visually-rich environment', *Perception and Psychophysics*, 1967, Vol. 2, pp. 249–55; G. Fisher and A. Lucas, 'Illusions in concrete

situations; 1. Introduction and demonstrations, *Ergonomics*, 1969, Vol. 12, pp. 11–24.

41 J. L. M. Dawson, 'Theory and research in cross-cultural psychology', *Bull. Brit. Psychol. Soc.*, 1971, Vol. 24, pp. 291–306.

42 W. C. Gogel, 'The effect of object familiarity on the perception of size and distance', *Quart. J. exp. Psychol.*, 1969, Vol. 21, pp. 239–47.

43 A. Smith, *Throw out Two Hands*, London: Allen & Unwin, 1963, p. 154.

44 D. Gray, *Rope Boy*, London: Gollancz, 1970, p. 72.

45 S. H. Bartley, *Perception in Everyday Life*, New York: Harper and Row, 1972, p. 7.

46 H. E. Ross, R. S. King and H. Snowden, 'Size and distance judgements in the vertical plane under water', *Psychol. Forsch.*, 1970, Vol. 33, pp. 155–64.

47 More detailed physical explanations can be found in: W. J. Humphreys, *Physics of the Air*, New York: Dover, 1964.

48 M. Minnaert, *Light and Colour in the Open Air* (translated by H. M. Kremer-Priest, revised by K. E. Brian Jay), London: Bell, 1959.

49 V. Cornish, *Scenery and the Sense of Sight*, Cambridge: Cambridge University Press, 1935, p. 44.

50 R. MacDougall, 'The subjective horizon', *Psych. Rev. Monogr. Suppl.*, 1903, Vol. 4, pp. 145–66.

51 For a review see I. P. Howard and W. B. Templeton, *Human Spatial Orientation*, London: Wiley, 1966, pp. 183–9.

52 The 'Electric Brae' (more properly known as 'Croy Brae') is situated on route A.719, between Ayr and Girvan, Ayrshire.

53 J. Nicklaus, *My 55 ways to Lower your Golf Score*, London: Hodder & Stoughton, 1965, p. 67.

54 R. Kammann, 'The over-estimation of vertical distance and slope and its role in the moon illusion', *Percept. Psychophys.*, 1967, Vol. 2, pp. 585–9.

55 R. B. Freeman, Jr., 'Ecological optics and visual slant', *Psychol. Rev.*, 1965, Vol. 72, pp. 501–4.

CHAPTER 4

Sound and Communication

Sound is almost as important to us as sight, and yet it receives much less attention in most textbooks. Changes in the environment probably cause as many auditory as visual distortions: some of the more noticeable effects are discussed in this chapter.

I *Pitch and the Doppler Effect*

Most town-dwellers will have noticed the Doppler effect: the ambulance or fire-engine rushes past sounding its siren, and the pitch suddenly drops as the vehicle passes. A similar effect occurs when the observer drives at speed past a stationary sound source.

This effect follows from the nature of soundwaves and the speed of sound. A sound is usually considered as a wave, travelling through a medium such as air. The distance between the crests of the waves is called the wavelength, and the height of the waves is known as the pressure, amplitude or intensity (Fig. 4.1). The velocity of sound is the rate at which the crests pass a stationary spot – normally about 344 metres per second at room temperature, reducing to about 331 m/s at freezing point. The frequency of a sound is the number of crests passing per second, and is inversely related to the wavelength. If f is the frequency, v the velocity, and λ the wavelength, then $f = \frac{v}{\lambda}$. If t is the time in seconds between each crest, then $t = \frac{\lambda}{v}$ and $f = \frac{1}{t}$.

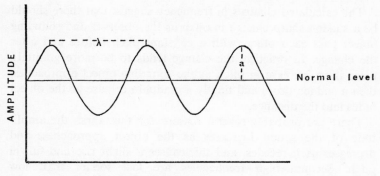

DISTANCE

FIGURE 4.1

The sound wave of a pure tone. The wavelength λ is the distance between the crests, and the amplitude a is the height of the crest above the mean level (the normal level when no wave is present).

The pitch of a sound depends mainly on its frequency, though it also increases slightly with the amplitude. Anything which increases the velocity of sound will also increase the frequency, and therefore raise the pitch. This can be done by raising the temperature of the air, or by changing the medium to one through which soundwaves travel faster (e.g. helium or water). The Doppler effect depends on a different principle: the velocity of the sounding object (relative to the observer) is added to, or subtracted from, the velocity of sound, with consequent altera- tion of the frequency received by the observer. Mathematically speaking, one could equally well say that the wavelength changes while the frequency remains unchanged (since $\lambda = \frac{v}{f}$); but, as far as the observer is concerned, there is a change in pitch which is approximately equivalent to the calculated change in frequency. If the observer is stationary and is approached by a sounding object of velocity u, then the received wavelength is $\frac{v-u}{f}$; or, alternatively, the received frequency is $\frac{fv}{v-u}$ (f being the original frequency, and v the speed of sound). Similarly, when the sound- ing object recedes, the received frequency is $\frac{fv}{v+u}$ – a lower pitch than when the object approaches.[1]

The calculated changes in frequency suggest that there should be a sudden sharp change in pitch as the observer and sounding object pass each other, with a constant pitch before and after the change. In practice, the change tends to be more gradual: there is an increase in pitch as the sounding object approaches, then a sudden drop, and finally a gradual decrease as the object fades into the distance.

There are probably several reasons for this. First, the amplitude of the sound increases as the object approaches, and decreases as it recedes, and this causes a slight rise and fall in pitch. Second, high frequencies are lost sooner than low frequencies as the distance increases, so that the high frequency components of a complex sound become more evident as the object passes the observer. Third, the approach velocity of the object is constant only if the observer is exactly in the path of the object: this is rarely the case, so the change in frequency is unlikely to be a simple step function as the object passes the observer.

II Pitch and the 'Donald Duck' Effect

The velocity of sound is affected by the medium in which it travels. Its speed increases in gases of low molecular weight, such as helium or hydrogen, producing a bizarre effect on the speech of anyone breathing such a gas. Divers working at depths below about 80 m usually breath an air mixture in which the nitrogen has been replaced by helium, to avoid problems of nitrogen narcosis (Ch. 2). This produces speech difficulties, whether the divers are attempting to talk through an underwater communication system, or are living in an underwater house supplied with oxy-helium.

The speech distortion is due to the fact that the increased velocity of sound increases the 'formants' of the voice (the maxima of the frequency spectrum), the increase being proportional to the change in the velocity of sound in the exhaled breath. The result is a squeaky 'Donald Duck' type of speech, which is very difficult to understand. Practice produces a small improvement, both for speakers and for listeners; but the learning is minimal. To aid communication, 'unscramblers' have been

manufactured which attempt to convert helium speech into something approaching normal speech. It is not sufficient to reduce
the component frequencies by a fixed number of cycles per
second – the difference must be proportional to each frequency.
One way of doing this is to play a tape-recording back at a
slower speed, but this has the disadvantage of distorting the time-
scale and making the speech unintelligible in a different way.
However, the correct time-scale can be preserved if a portion of
each sound is discarded while the recording is slowed down.[2]
Another method is to break the speech signal into a number of
frequency bands, and to reduce the frequency of each by a
different fixed amount; in this case, the larger the number of
bands, the better the approximation. Unscramblers can work
well at atmospheric pressure, given the expected proportions
of oxygen and helium. In practice, unscramblers are normally
used at greater-than-atmospheric pressure, when they are not so
successful.[3] Pressure causes additional complications, because it
transposes the formants in a different way from helium.[4] With
the increase in deep diving, and in pressure chamber simulations,
better unscramblers are likely to be developed.

III *Echoes and Echolocation*

Echoes are due to the reflection of sound by objects. When a
soundwaves meets an object, the behaviour of the wave depends
on the relative sizes of the object and the wavelength. If the
wave is relatively large, it will flow round the object, like a sea-
wave round a post; if small, it will be reflected from the object.
The wavelengths of light are very short, so that light can
normally be considered as rays travelling in straight lines. Soundwaves, on the other hand, are about the same size as many
objects; they show mixed behaviour, and it is sometimes more
convenient to consider them as waves than as rays.

Sounds are reflected from large objects in a similar manner
to light rays from a mirror, the angle of incidence being equal
to the angle of reflection. The most familiar example of this
is the echo off a distant wall or mountain (Fig. 4.2), where the
echo sounds loudest if one stands in the direction of the reflected
sound. The echo of one's own voice will, of course, be loudest

F

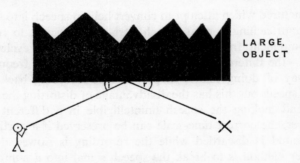

FIGURE 4.2

Echoes off a large object. The angle of incidence (i) is equal to the angle of reflection (r). The echo sounds louder from X than from other directions.

if one is perpendicular to the wall. The echoes from small objects (Fig. 4.3) scatter in all directions, though they are slightly louder towards the direction of the original sound.

Echoes and reverberations occur frequently indoors, and to a lesser extent outside; but we scarcely notice them. We are most aware of them after a short sharp noise such as a gun shot, followed by an echo from a distant mountain. This is because we need a slight pause between a sound and its echo for the echo to be detectable. Usually the echo is reflected back so quickly that it intermingles with the original sound. For example, if a sound lasting one second extends 344 m through the air, it must be reflected from an object more than half that distance away (172 m) to send an echo back to the source *after* the original sound has ended.

Echoes are usually masked because the original sound continues too long. However, we also fail to notice echoes at the end of words and sounds, even though the original sounds last for only a fraction of a second. It seems that the brain suppresses echoes at the end of sounds but not at the start. This is obvious if a tape-recording is played backwards – most backwards words appear to start with a swooshing noise, which is quite inaudible at the end of normal words. Distant echoes out of doors can be heard because they are outside the suppressor period. This suppressor period lasts for about 50 msec., and is

probably the same thing as the 'Haas' or 'Precedence Effect':
when two similar sounds occur within this period, a single sound
is heard, which appears to be located at the source of the first
sound (or the louder or nearer sound, which is usually also the
first sound).[5]

If the distance between the sound source and the reflecting
object is very great, the time difference between the original
sound and the echo can be used to calculate the distance of the
object. Sound travelling at 344 metres per second will return as
an echo from an object 344 m away in two seconds: the distance
of the echoing object in metres can therefore be calculated by
multiplying the number of elapsing seconds by 172.

When the echoing object is close, the echo falls within the
suppressor period: it is not consciously heard as an echo, and
cannot be used to calculate distances. Nevertheless, the echo
makes an appreciable difference to the quality of a sound.
Blind people, and trained sighted people, can sense the presence
of objects by this difference. This ability was originally called
'facial vision', though Dresslar suggested in 1893 that it was
due to auditory cues rather than to some unknown skin sense.[6]

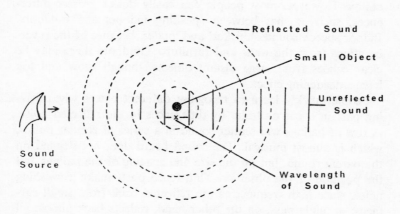

FIGURE 4.3

Echoes off a small object. When a beam of sound has a wavelength
greater than that of the object, the scattered sound goes in all directions. It is slightly louder in the direction of the original sound. (After
D. R. Griffin, *Echoes of Bats and Men*, London: Heinemann, 1959.)

The importance of auditory cues was later confirmed,[7] and the ability is now known as 'echolocation', 'echo-detection' or 'sonar'.

Echolocation is used most effectively by certain animals, such as bats and porpoises, which are able both to emit and to hear very high pitched sounds.[8] Sounds of high frequency – or short wavelength – produce the best echo resolution for very small targets: sounds of long wavelength tend to flow round small objects instead of being sharply reflected. Human beings cannot hear very high frequencies, but can become extremely skilful at echo-detection when using high-pitched taps and clicks. They can learn both to detect the presence of objects, and to distinguish between different sorts of objects. They can detect the presence of targets subtending an angle as small as 3·5° (3·8 cm at a distance of 61 cm); discriminate difference ratios of 1·11/1 in the radii of two flat disks presented successively; distinguish between a circle, square and triangle of the same surface area; and locate the position of a flat target very precisely, with or without head movements.[9] They can also discriminate between different types of material, on the basis of the differences in reflected sound.[10]

Considerable practice is needed to attain such a high level of ability. However, most people can easily detect grosser differences, such as that between speaking indoors and outdoors. Indoor speech sounds 'thicker' and louder, because of the reverberations from the walls and furniture. Outdoors there may be clear echoes from large distant objects, though snow and fog have a deadening effect.

People quickly learn to recognise different places when driving past in a car or train, by differences in the reflected noise. A row of palings will scatter sound in a series of regular pulses, which is almost musical. The sound heard does not depend on the parent sound, but on the size and spacing of the palings and the position of the observer. Thin fence posts make a swishing noise, since high frequencies are reflected back from small surfaces; an underpass, on the other hand, reflects back almost all frequencies, causing a steady roar. Train drivers can recognise places on their route, and detect differences in speed of travel, from tape-recordings of the sound.[11]

IV   *Temperature, Wind and Refraction*

The previous section was concerned with echoes – the reflection of soundwaves at a sharp density-gradient. When a soundwave meets a gradual density-gradient, most of the sound is refracted rather than reflected: it is transmitted through the medium at a different angle.

Refraction is an important factor out of doors, because the air is rarely completely still or of constant density. Density-gradients are often caused by temperature changes, one of these being the decrease of air temperature with increase in height. If a sound originates from the earth's warm surface layer, its wave front is refracted upwards (its velocity being greater in the lower and warmer air). The effect of this is that the sound becomes faint at other points on the surface of the earth, but is heard more clearly from above. Sometimes there is a temperature inversion, and the opposite effect occurs. This may happen when there is a ground frost at night, and the temperature is colder just above the earth's surface than it is higher up. In this case, a large pro-portion of the sound is refracted downwards and confined within the inversion layer, enabling sounds to carry very well close to the ground. The effect can be enhanced if one shouts along a river with steep banks: the banks and the river reflect the sound, while the inversion layer refracts it, so that the sound is funnelled along a tube instead of being lost in the open air. Occasionally, acoustical mirages occur: when there are bands of air a few metres thick of different temperatures, the sound wave is refracted in such a way that it appears to come from more than one source.[1]

The wind is a further cause of distortion. The speed of the wind increases with its distance from the ground, distorting the shape of the wave front (Fig. 4.4). When a person shouts with the wind, his voice is driven downwards, and he is heard more clearly at ground level; but when he shouts against the wind, the opposite is true. Sounds coming from windward are some-times heard extremely clearly on the leeward side of a mountain: the wind flows roughly parallel to the mountain side, blowing the wave front over the top of the mountain, and its increased

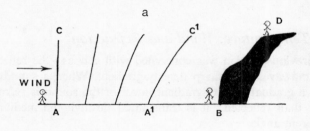

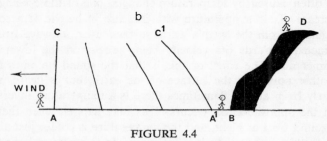

FIGURE 4.4

Refraction of sound by the wind. The wave front AC becomes A^1C^1, which is heard more clearly at ground level (B) when shouting with the wind (a); and more clearly at height (D) when shouting against the wind (b).

speed at height drives the front down into a focus in the leeward valley.

Rock climbers often have great difficulty in hearing each other. This is mainly due to wind carrying the voices away, and to overhanging rocks between the climbers which reflect the sound. Occasionally, refraction at temperature gradients contributes to their difficulties. A third climber standing some way back from the rock-face can usually shout effectively to both the lower and the higher climber, showing that the difficulty arises only near the face. Sometimes voices are lost both upwards and downwards, and sometimes in one direction only.

Fortunately, the series of calls between two roped climbers is fairly stereotyped,[12] and it may not matter much if the voices are unclear. Sound distortions can be more serious for ships: they have been known to collide with other ships, or founder on the rocks, because fog-horn signals appear to come from the wrong direction, or are not heard at all.

V   *The Loss of Sound with Distance*

Soundwaves gradually disappear as they travel, their energy being lost in heating the air. The loss is greater for high than low frequencies. In a still and homogeneous medium, the sound intensity varies inversely with the square of the distance. This loss of intensity is known as the 'inverse square loss', or the '1/R loss'. When expressed in decibels,[13] the loss between two distances is equal to $20 \log_{10} (R/R_o)$, when R_o is the shorter distance and R the longer distance.[14] For each doubling of the distance, the intensity loss increases by 6 db (since the logarithm of 2 is about 0·3).

In practice, the loss of intensity is rarely as steady as this equation implies. Indoors the sound is reflected off the walls and furniture, producing a louder and more complex sound than out of doors. If a pure tone of suitable wavelength for the size of the room is played indoors, the reflected sound from the walls can combine with the sound from the source to give areas of maximum and minimum intensity. The maxima and minima are called 'standing waves', and the distance between the maxima is one half wavelength. Concert halls, of course, are carefully designed to avoid dead and loud spots, and to ensure the best amount of reverberation for all frequencies when the hall is full of people.

Out of doors, near the earth's surface, sounds usually dissipate slightly more rapidly than the inverse square law implies. This is probably due to the turbulence of the lower air – eddies help to disperse the sound, and reduce its intensity. Some interesting anomalies arise in the case of balloonists, and climbers up high mountains, when they listen to sounds from the earth's surface: they report that they can hear and understand people on the ground who cannot hear them. There are probably several reasons for this, apart from obvious explanations concerned with wind direction. One possible factor is that the density of the atmosphere is reduced with height, so that the balloonist's voice carries less energy than on the ground; however, this difference is slight, and unlikely to be very important. Another difference is that the balloonist hears both the direct and the reflected portions of the voice below him coming from approximately the same direction, thus increasing the loudness and clarity, while the ground observer hears the balloonist's voice directly from overhead and reflected mainly from the ground. However, the most important difference is probably that the balloonist has a silent background, and the ground observer a noisy one: the signal-to-noise ratio is higher for the balloonist, and this is one of the main factors determining the audibility of signals. It must be important in the case of the balloonist, because he can often hear the earth-echo of his own voice when the ground observers cannot hear him.[1]

VI *Loudness Constancy*

There is no doubt that the physical intensity of a sound diminishes with distance – but how does this affect the *apparent* loudness? In practice there is some degree of 'loudness constancy': the apparent loudness of a sound does not decrease as fast as would be expected on the basis of physical measurements. Loudness constancy is not complete, any more than size constancy is complete; there is some loss in apparent loudness with distance, just as there is some decrease in the apparent size of objects with distance.

One must have some idea of the distance of the sound source, in order to compensate appropriately for the loss of intensity. The knowledge of distance may be obtained by visual cues, or by auditory cues, or by knowledge gained previously about the likely source of such a sound. Sometimes one makes errors, particularly when sleepy or inattentive: a small noise in the bedroom may sound like a loud explosion outside, causing the drowsy occupant to wake with a start. Sir David Brewster was well aware of this when he wrote his *Letters on Natural Magic*, around 1832: 'There is no species of deception more irresistible in its effects than that which arises from the uncertainty with which we judge of the direction of sounds. Every person must have noticed how a sound in their own ears is often mistaken for some loud noise moderated by the distance from which it is supposed to come; and the sportsman must have frequently been surprised at the existence of musical sounds humming remotely in the extended heath, when it was only the wind sounding in the barrel of his gun.'[15]

Few experiments on loudness constancy appear to have been undertaken, though Mohrmann published some measurements in 1939. Mohrmann used only a small range of distances (up to 750 cm), so few conclusions about the change of apparent loudness with distance can be drawn from his data. However, by using different test conditions, he was able to show that loudness constancy was greater for complex sounds (such as speech and music), than for pure tones; and was greater when visual cues were available, than when subjects were tested in the dark.[16]

VII *Auditory Distance Perception*

Relatively little is known about the auditory cues to distance, but current knowledge on the subject has been reviewed by Coleman.[17]

Cues are either monaural, in which case they are derived from the alteration of sound by its passage through the medium; or they are binaural, and derived from the geometry of the head and the behaviour of sound waves near the head. The main monaural cue is the loss of intensity with distance. This, of course, raises the problem as to whether the apparent loudness determines the apparent distance, or *vice versa*. The answer must be that both are interdependent, and that both are also partly determined by other cues. Loudness, or apparent intensity, can be a cue to distance only if the observer has some idea of the 'normal' loudness of the sound at a known distance; he must therefore use other cues to identify the nature of the sound. A further monaural distance cue may be a change in the frequency spectrum of complex sounds, though the nature of the changes at different distances is controversial. Indoors, the change in the ratio of direct to reflected sound can be an important cue – nearer sources have a larger proportion of direct sound. Binaural cues can probably be used for sound sources off to one side of the observer, since the binaural intensity differences and binaural phase differences (see Section VIII) vary at different distances. The change in binaural cues is probably important only at close distances. It seems that when all the distance cues are available, auditory distance perception is quite good; but that no cue in isolation is very effective.

If the source of a sound is straight ahead, and all distance cues are removed, people localise the apparent source at the nearest reasonable location. This is known as the *proximity-image effect*.[18] Gardner[19] found that subjects were unable to tell the distance of speech coming from a loudspeaker, when the sound came from straight ahead in an anechoic chamber. However, distance discrimination improved if the subjects were allowed to make small head movements, or to keep the head fixed at an angle. Discrimination improved further if live speech rather than a loudspeaker source was used.

VIII *Auditory Directional Perception*

The cues used in discriminating the direction of a sound are better understood than those for distance. As with distance, we rely a good deal on vision and common sense. This is essential, because sounds do not always travel in straight lines – they bend round obstacles and reflect off broad surfaces, so that they no longer indicate the direction of a source. Nevertheless there are some useful auditory cues to direction.

The cues are mainly binaural: they depend on the slight differences in the auditory stimuli received by the two ears. Provided the sound source is off-centre, there will be differences between the left and right ear in intensity, time of incidence, phase, and complexity. The intensity difference arises mainly because the farther ear is in the 'sound shadow' cast by the head; low frequency sounds are relatively unaffected because they bend round the head easily, but high frequency sounds have wavelengths sufficiently small to be reflected by the head. Temporal cues operate at the beginning and end of a sound, and whenever the sound changes character: obviously the nearer ear receives the changed signal first. In the case of a steady tone the temporal cue becomes a phase difference, the regular peaks and troughs of the soundwave being out of register in the two ears. For high frequency tones the phase difference is difficult to interpret: high tones have wavelengths of the order of the distance between the two ears, so that a phase difference is either lacking or may reverse its apparent direction. Complexity differences occur only for compound tones and noises. The sound shadow cast by the head is frequency-selective: the screened ear receives sounds with the high frequencies attenuated, with a resulting difference in *timbre*, or quality. Thus the cues that are used depend on the type of sound: high tones depend mainly on intensity differences and low tones on phase differences; while complex tones depend on intensity, time and *timbre*.

If the sound source is directly in front, behind, up or down, the cues are the same for both ears, and the listener has difficulty in distinguishing between these directions. However, head movements can help;[20] and the flaps of the outer ear may also play a part in the case of high-pitched tones, by shielding different proportions of the sound in different directions.[21] It is presumably cues of this type which are used by people who are completely deaf in one ear, yet have quite good directional localisation.[22]

The angular difference in direction which most people can discriminate lies between about 1–10°, depending on the actual direction of the sound and its frequency. People are better at discriminating between 'left' and 'right' than 'front' and 'back'; so discrimination is best in the region straight ahead of the subject, and poor (over 40°) at the side. It is also best when the frequency lies between about 250 and 1,000 cycles per second – the region where differences in time of arrival are the main cue; at higher frequencies intensity differences are more important, but with less effective results.[23]

Auditory localisation being imprecise, we tend to rely heavily on visual cues in judging the exact source of a sound. This accounts for the success of ventriloquists – we tend to associate the speech sounds with moving rather than still lips. In some laboratory experiments a conflict is artificially introduced between visual and auditory locational cues, by the use of distorting lenses or a distorting auditory system;[24] in such experiments vision tends to dominate, just as it does when vision and touch conflict. Similarly, when touch and hearing conflict, the tactile and other bodily cues usually dominate:[25] the auditory directional system is weak, and rarely wins in conflict with other senses.

Conflict of this sort is not confined to laboratory experiments. The echoes and other distortions already described can confuse listeners as to the true source of a sound. Divers are particularly unfortunate, as they face a double distortion: the facemask distorts the visual cues to the sound source (Ch. 3), and the increased speed of sound in water distorts the auditory cues (see Section IX). Doubless, divers adapt to both sensory distortions; but no work seems to have been done on this double problem.

Errors of auditory localisation can be due to a different cause: the listener may fail to make adequate allowance for the orientation of his head or body. Compensation for lateral turning of the head is quite good,[26] but errors can arise due to body tilt.[27] Errors can also be caused by false sensations of bodily movement or orientation, due to unusual accelerative forces: such errors are known as the *audiogyral* and *audiogravic* illusions (Ch. 6).

IX   *Auditory Localisation Under Water*

Divers have considerable difficulty in locating the source of a sound under water. This can be dangerous when the source is an overhead motor boat, and the diver wishes to surface well away from the boat. Sudden and unlocatable noises can add to the diver's other anxieties, particularly since the noise may appear to originate very close to the head.[28]

The diver's difficulties have two main causes. One cause is that sound travels about four and a half times faster in water than in air, so that all frequencies are effectively higher, and phase differences are more difficult to detect. The other main cause is that the intensity difference is reduced, because the head has little shadowing effect under water – the sound waves pass through it with little loss of energy. Bauer and Torick[29] have suggested that the diver should wear earphones on long antennae in order to restore the phase difference; but for normal diving purposes such an encumbrance is not worth the trouble.

Contrary to popular opinion, most divers do have some ability to locate the source of a sound.[30-44] Under favourable conditions they can detect an angular difference in direction of about 7·5° for broadband noise, increasing to about 11·5° for noise of a narrow frequency range.[37] The equivalent location threshold for broadband noise in air is about 2°. Since there is a reduction in the phase and intensity differences, fewer cues to bodily orientation (Ch. 5), and a general deterioration of performance under water (Ch. 2), the observed thresholds are remarkably fine. Divers probably make use of head movements,[35] or of other monaural cues. They may also improve their directional sensitivity by wearing a neoprene diving hood, which enhances the intensity difference between the two ears.[30, 31, 35] However, a hood does have the disadvantage of reducing absolute hearing thresholds in water.[38]

As the head is moved around under water, the change in binaural cues is different from the equivalent change in air. This deformation of the 'binaural image' with head movements is logically similar to the rubbery transformation of an optically distorted image when the observer moves around. Sounds under water initially seem to be located nearer than they are in reality because of the increased rate of transmission of soundwaves. Divers probably adapt to this distortion to some extent, since they can obtain information about it from head movements or from a discrepancy between visual and auditory cues. No underwater experiments seem to have been done; but auditory spatial adaptation has been demonstrated during some laboratory experiments in air.[39]

X   Sensitivity to Sounds Under Water

Soundwaves travel poorly between air and water, most of the sound being reflected at the change of medium. A diver cannot hear sounds originating in air, unless they are extremely loud. Sounds which originate under water, on the other hand, are transmitted very well. The diver's world is often very noisy – he may hear the throbbing of an outboard motor, the splashing of swimmers, the snapping of shrimps and the noise of divers moving equipment around; but loudest of all is the regular hiss of inhaled air and the roar of exhaust bubbles, which can drown all other noises.

However, the diver's world is not as noisy as it might be, since the human ear is less efficient in water than in air. The ear converts sound pressure waves into nervous signals, and does this mainly by means of the impedance (density) difference between the sound-carrying medium and the various parts of the auditory system. In the air, the sound is conducted both through the eardrum system and through the bones of the head. In water, it is not clear precisely what mechanism is used, the impedance of soft tissue being almost the same as that of water, and the impedance of bone being only slightly greater. Some evidence suggests that bone conduction is probably the main mechanism: for example, subjects with middle-ear conduction deficiencies perform as well as normal subjects under water, while those with bone conduction deficiencies continue to perform worse.[40] However, the fact that binaural localisation is possible does seem to imply that some useful eardrum hearing must occur, in addition to bone conduction.

Auditory sensitivity in water has been measured over a wide range of frequencies by several experimenters.[38, 40, 41] There is a difference of about 20–30 db between the lowest and highest values found by different experimenters; but there is general agreement that the finest sensitivity occurs at a frequency of about 1,000 cycles per second, with decreasing sensitivity at higher and lower frequencies. At the optimal frequency, divers with normal hearing can detect pure tones having an intensity of about 61–64 db.[40] A neoprene diving hood worn over the ears reduces sensitivity by a further 20–40 db;[38, 42] and further losses occur if the diver breathes in or out while listening, or fails to clear his ears properly.

Diving at quite shallow depths, then, is likely to reduce sensitivity by at least 60 db, and probably more. If the diver goes deep, and breathes air or oxyhelium under considerable pressure, there may be further loss. Pressure-chamber experiments, using compressed air, suggest that transmission through the middle-ear system is seriously reduced – so, if this system is of any use under water, there may be an increased hearing loss at depth.[43] In practice, oxyhelium seems to transmit sounds worse than compressed air, causing a further loss of about 5 db in underwater thresholds.[44]

XI *Communication Under Water*

If divers wish to speak to each other under water, or communicate with the surface, they have several problems. The speaker must be able to produce intelligible speech signals; the signals must be conveyed to the listener; and the listener must be able to hear them. All of these stages are impaired under water.

There are basically three types of communication system which divers can use: 'hard-line', 'acoustic', and 'modulated'. A hard-line system is a closed system, comparable to a telephone, which includes a microphone, a cable for transmitting the signal, and a receiver or earphone. An acoustic system transduces speech directly into the water through a microphone and underwater loudspeaker: the signal can be heard without a receiver by any diver within range. A modulated system is more complex: an ultrasonic carrier-frequency is transduced into the water after being modulated in some manner by the speech signal, and is then decoded into speech by the receiver; the sender must carry a microphone, power module, amplifier, modulator and underwater transducer, while the listener must carry an appropriate receiver and demodulator system. A particular problem with this system is to find a type of modulation that resists 'multiple-path distortion' – the distortion that occurs in water of moderate depth when signals are reflected off both the bottom and the surface, so that the reflected signals reach the listener at slightly different times from different directions. A listener on land can normally distinguish between a signal and its echoes by knowing the direction of the source, but he is less able to do this when listening to a receiver system under water.

A problem common to all systems is that of the initial production of the speech signal. The diver has to speak into a full facemask, or into a mouthmask attached to the demand valve. The mask can be regarded as a closed cavity with high impedance, giving little transmission through its walls.[45] Larger masks allow better speech, but carry an added risk of a build-up of CO_2 in the dead-space. Some divers are capable of producing their own 'free acoustic' system, by speaking directly into the water, with or without a normal mouthpiece in their mouth: such speech can be heard at short distances, and understood by well-practised partners. Most, however, need a microphone inside some kind of mouthmask.

The final common problem is the poor hearing of the diver, in competition with all the other underwater noises. The two divers must synchronise their breathing if they wish to communicate with one another, because the breathing noises are extremely loud. Once extraneous noises have been eliminated, speech reception thresholds are quite predictable from other auditory thresholds in water.[46]

The end result of all these difficulties is that no communication system currently available is more than 72 per cent intelligible during diver-to-diver tests, though diver-to-surface communication can be quite satisfactory.[47] Divers working together on a construction task may, in fact, be quicker and more accurate without a speech communication system than with one![48] Divers can generally make themselves understood by a series of nods, taps, kicks and other gestures. The finer nuances of eye-contact are rarely possible, but divers who know each other well usually evolve an elaborate system of gestures. When the information is complicated, messages written on a slate are more reliable than speech.

Divers are usually taught how to communicate with the surface by pulling on a rope suspended from a boat.[49] Both diver and tender need considerable practice before they can operate the system with any success – it is often very difficult for the tender to count the correct number of 'pulls' (long heaves) and 'bells' (quick tugs), and to distinguish these from accidental snagging of the rope. Divers are also taught the use of standard hand signals, and beginners are usually very conscientious about using them. They dutifully signal to each other 'Are you all right?', 'Yes, I am all right', as they descend; but experienced divers tend not to bother. Hand signals are often as redundant as 'Good morning, nice weather' – they convey reassurance, or good manners, rather than important information. An experienced diver usually notices if his partner is unhappy, and does not

PLATE 5

The Electric Brae, Ayrshire, Scotland. (a) Apparently uphill but truly downhill view. (b) Apparently downhill but truly uphill view.

PLATE 6

Divers attempting to point to the vertical. (a) Upright. (b) Inverted. (Photographs by N. V. Sills. From H. E. Ross *et al.*, *Aerospace Med.*, 1969, Vol. 40, pp. 728–32.)

need to be told what is wrong. Hand signals can thus serve different functions according to the level of experience: they can convey 'obvious' information to novices, and be reserved for more complex information when both partners are experienced.

XII *Communication on the Road*

Drivers, like divers, are taught to use a lot of hand signals (or indicator signals) before passing their test; and they, too, use fewer signals as their experience increases.[50] This may be because many signals are redundant; they are a waste of effort from the sender's point of view, and they overload other drivers with unnecessary information. Some signals are best avoided because they are ambiguous: for example, flashing headlights can mean 'Do go ahead, I'll wait', or 'Wait, I'm going first'; and a slowing-down hand signal can mean 'Do overtake me' or 'I am slowing down because of some obstruction, and it is not safe for you to overtake me'. A signal which can hardly be avoided, but is nevertheless ambiguous, is a right flashing indicator (or right hand signal): this can mean 'I am turning right' or 'I am overtaking' or 'I am moving into a faster lane, and staying there' or 'I am starting up after parking'. Cohen[50] interviewed 225 drivers of various sorts, and they described over 50 different signals as being appropriate for only 13 manœuvres, with 17 for 'I do not think it is safe for you to overtake me'. He found that the signals which drivers actually gave at roundabouts were particularly variable: of drivers turning left, 10 per cent signalled right, 22 per cent left, 68 per cent not at all; and of drivers going straight on, 39 per cent signalled right, 4 per cent left, and 57 per cent not at all.

Decisions have to be made quickly while driving, and there is no time to give or interpret a complex set of signals. It is probably best to use only a few standard signals, and to use them consistently. Part of the trouble arises because drivers are not sure where to go, and cannot make up their minds quickly enough. This subject raises the question of orientation and navigation, which is continued in the next chapter.

NOTES

1   A more detailed explanation of these phenomena can be found in: W. J. Humphreys, *Physics of the air*, New York: Dover, 1964.
2   W. R. Stover, 'Techniques for correcting helium speech distortion', *J. Acoust. Soc. Amer.*, 1967, Vol. 41, pp. 70–4.
3   H. Hollien and J. Malone, 'On-line evaluation of three HeO_2 speech unscramblers', *J. Acoust. Soc. Amer.*, 1969, Vol. 46, p. 82.
4   G. M. Fandt, J. Lindqvist, B. Sonesson and H. Hollien, 'Speech distortion at high pressures', in *Underwater Physiology*, edited by C. J. Lambertsen, New York: Academic Press, 1971, pp. 293–9.
5   M. B. Gardner, 'Historical background of the Haas and/or Precedence Effect', *J. Acoust. Soc. Amer.*, 1968, Vol. 43, pp. 1243–8.
6   F. B. Dresslar, 'On the pressure sense of the drum of the ear and facial vision', *Amer. J. Psychol.*, 1893, Vol. 5, pp. 344–50.
7   M. Supin, M. Cotzin and K. M. Dallenbach, ' "Facial vision", the perception of obstacles by the blind', *Amer. J. Psychol.*, 1944, Vol. 57, pp. 133–83.
8   D. R. Griffin, *Echoes of Bats and Men*, London: Heinemann, 1959.
9   C. E. Rice, 'Human echo perception', *Science*, 1967, Vol. 155, pp. 656–64; C. E. Rice and S. H. Feinstein, 'Sonar system of the blind: size discrimination', *Science*, 1965, Vol. 148, pp. 1107–8; C. E. Rice, S. H. Feinstein and R. J. Schusterman, 'Echo detection ability of the blind: size and distance factors', *J. exp. Psychol.*, 1965, Vol. 70, pp. 246–51.
10 W. N. Kellogg, 'Sonar system of the blind', *Science*, 1962, Vol. 137, pp. 399–404.
11 L. Buck, 'Auditory perception of position and speed', *J. Applied Psychology*, 1963, Vol. 47, pp. 177–83.
12 H. MacInnes, *Climbing*, Edinburgh: Scottish Youth Hostels Association, 1963, p. 18.
13 The decibel scale is a logarithmic scale in which 0 represents the threshold of hearing (at a sound intensity of $0·0002$ dyne per cm^2), 50 a quiet conversation, 100 a loud motor horn, and 130 the threshold for pain. The scale is derived by taking 10 times the common logarithm of the ratio between the intensities of the sound in question and a reference sound (usually the threshold intensity). If the intensity of a sound is doubled, the loudness in decibels is increased by only 3 units. This logarithmic scale corresponds well with *apparent loudness*, rather than physical intensity.
14 This equation is derived from the fact that the ratio of the sound intensities at the two distances (I_o/I) is equal to the inverse of the ratio of the squares of the distances (i.e. to R^2/R_o^2). The intensity difference in decibels is given by $10 \log_{10} (I_o/I)$, which is equal to $10 \log_{10} (R/R_o)^2$ or $20 \log_{10} (R/R_o)$.
15 D. Brewster, *Letters on Natural Magic*, London: Murray, 1832, pp. 164–5.
16 K. Mohrmann, 'Lautheitskonstanz im Entfernungswechsel', *Zeitschrift für Psychologie*, 1939, Vol. 145, pp. 145–99.

17   P. D. Coleman, 'An analysis of cues to auditory depth perception in free space', *Psychol. Bull.*, 1963, Vol. 60, pp. 302–15.

18   M. B. Gardner, 'Proximity image effect in sound localization', *J. Acoust. Soc. Amer.*, 1968, Vol. 43, p. 163.

19   M. B. Gardner, 'Distance estimation of $0°$ or apparent $0°$ – orientated speech signals in anechoic space', *J. Acoust. Soc. Amer.*, 1969, Vol. 45, pp. 47–53.

20   W. R. Thurlow and P. S. Runge, 'Effect of induced head movements on localization of direction of sounds', *J. Acoust. Soc. Amer.*, 1967, Vol. 42, pp. 480–93.

21   H. J. Fisher and S. J. Freedman, 'The role of the pinna in auditory localization', *J. Aud. Res.*, 1968, Vol. 8, pp. 15–26.

22   J. R. Angell and W. Fite, 'The monaural localization of sound', *Psych. Rev.*, 1901, Vol. 8, pp. 449–56; L. B. W. Jongkees and R. A. v.d.Veer, 'On directional sound localization in unilateral deafness and its explanation', *Acta Oto-Laryng.*, 1958, Vol. 49, pp. 119–131; R. G. Butler and R. F. Naunton, 'The effect of stimulus sensation level on the directional hearing of unilaterally deafened persons', *J. Sp. Hear. Res.*, 1964, Vol. 7, pp. 15–25; D. R. Perrott and L. Elfner, 'Monoural localization', *J. Aud. Res.*, 1968, Vol. 8, pp. 185–93.

23   A. W. Mills, 'On the minimum audible angle', *J. Acoust. Soc. Amer.*, 1958, Vol. 30, pp. 237–46.

24   H. A. Witkin, S. Wapner and T. Leventhal, 'Sound localization with conflicting visual and auditory cues', *J. exp. Psychol.*, 1952, Vol. 43, pp. 58–67.

25   G. H. Fisher, 'Spatial localization by the blind', *Amer. J. Psychol.*, 1964, Vol. 77, pp. 2–14.

26   R. H. Day, 'Perceptual constancy of auditory direction', *Nature*, 1968, Vol. 219, pp. 501–2.

27   P. R. Comalli and M. W. Altshuler, 'Effect of body tilt on auditory localization', *Percept. Mot. Skills*, 1971, Vol. 32, pp. 723–6.

28   S. Kitagawa and Y. Shintaku, 'Direction perception and subjective auditory perception line', *Acta Oto-Laryngol.*, 1957, Vol. 47, pp. 431–43.

29   B. B. Bauer and E. L. Torick, 'Experimental studies in underwater directional communication', *J. Acoust. Soc. Amer.*, 1966, Vol. 39, pp. 25–34.

30   J. M. Ide, 'Signalling and homing by underwater sound: For small craft and commando swimmers', Rep. No. 19, U.S. Naval Research Laboratory, Washington, D.C., 1944.

31   S. H. Feinstein, 'Human hearing under water: Are things as bad as they seem?' *J. Acoust. Soc. Amer.*, 1966, Vol. 40, pp. 1561–2.

32   S. Anderson and J. Christensen, 'Underwater sound localization in man', *J. Aud. Res.*, 1969, Vol. 9, pp. 358–64.

33   H. Hollien, 'Underwater sound localization: Preliminary information', *J. Acoust. Soc. Amer.*, 1969, Vol. 46, pp. 124–5.

34   T. Leggiere, J. McAniff, H. Schenck and J. van Ryzin, 'Sound localization and homing in divers', *Mar. Tech. Soc. J.*, 1969, Vol. 4, pp. 27–34.

35 B. Ray, 'Directional hearing by divers', *Underwater Ass. Rep.*, 1969, Vol. 4, pp. 49–52.

36 H. Hollien, J. L. Lauer and P. Paul, 'Additional data on underwater sound localization', *J. Acoust. Soc. Amer.*, 1970, Vol. 27, pp. 127–8.

37 S. H. Feinstein, *The acuity and precision of underwater sound localization*, Ph.D. Dissertation, Dalhousie University, Nova Scotia, 1971.

38 W. E. Montague and J. F. Strickland, 'Sensitivity of the water-immersed ear to high- and low-level tones', *J. Acoust. Soc. Amer.*, 1961, Vol. 33, pp. 1376–81.

39 D. R. Perrott, L. F. Elfner and J. L. Homick, 'Auditory spatial adaptation', *Perception and Psychophysics*, 1969, Vol. 5, pp. 189–92; H. H. Mikaelian, 'Adaptation to rearranged ear-hand coordination', *Percept. Mot. Skills*, 1969, Vol. 28, pp. 147–50.

40 P. F. Smith, 'Underwater hearing in man: 1. Sensitivity', Rep. No. 569, U.S. Naval Submarine Medical Center, Groton, Conn., 1969.

41 P. M. Hamilton, 'Underwater hearing thresholds', *J. Acoust. Soc. Amer.*, 1957, Vol. 29, pp. 792–4; W. N. Wainwright, 'Comparison of hearing thresholds in air and in water', *J. Acoust. Soc. Amer.*, 1958, Vol. 30, pp. 1025–9; J. F. Brandt and H. Hollien, 'Underwater hearing thresholds in man', *J. Acoust. Soc. Amer.*, 1967, Vol. 42, pp. 966–71.

42 R. J. Bogert, 'Attenuation of sound by neoprene diving helmet', U.S.N./U.S.L. Calibration Memo 2568–2610, 7 January 1964.

43 E. Fluur and J. Adolfson, 'Hearing in hyperbaric air', *Aerospace Med.*, 1966, Vol. 37, pp. 783–5.

44 J. F. Brandt, 'The effect of depth and content of the middle ear cavity on underwater hearing thresholds', *J. Acoust. Soc. Amer.*, 1967, Vol. 42, p. 1149.

45 B. Ray, 'Voice communication between divers', *Underwater Ass. Rep.*, 1966–67, Vol. 2, pp. 47–51.

46 J. F. Brandt and H. Hollien, 'Underwater speech reception thresholds and discrimination', *J. Aud. Res.*, 1968, Vol. 8, pp. 71–80.

47 H. Hollien, R. F. Coleman and H. Rothman, 'Evaluation of diver communication systems by a diver-to-diver technique', *Institute of Electrical and Electronic Engineers Transactions on Communication Technology*, 1971, Vol. 19, pp. 403–9.

48 H. Hollien, H. Rothman, P. Hollien and G. C. Tolhurst, 'Effectiveness of work by divers with and without voice communication', *J. Acoust. Soc. Amer.*, 1971, Vol. 50, p. 131.

49 *British Sub Aqua Club Diving Manual*, London: British Sub Aqua Club, 1972 (7th edition).

50 J. Cohen and B. Preston, *Causes and Prevention of Road Accidents*, London: Faber & Faber, 1968.

CHAPTER 5

Orientation and Geographical Perception

This chapter is mainly concerned with how we know which way is up, and how we find our way around. It considers the types of cues that we use in various environments, and the mistakes we make when the cues are inadequate or contradictory.

I Cues for Vertical Orientation

A man standing on earth normally has several sorts of cues available to him, all indicating the direction of the gravitational vertical. These cues can be subdivided into three main classes: visual – from the alignment of plants, buildings and other objects; vestibular – from the sensory signals originating in the utricle and semicircular canals of the inner ear; and tactile-kinaesthetic – from the pressure and joint receptors in various parts of the body.[1]

The relative importance of these different sorts of cues is controversial – probably because it is not possible to run comparable experiments removing each cue in turn. It is easy to remove visual cues, by testing in the dark or using blind subjects. It is possible to remove vestibular cues, by testing under zero gravity or by using subjects with damaged vestibular systems. Tactile-kinaesthetic cues can be reduced (but not totally eliminated) by zero gravity, immersion in water, or anaesthetisation of the surface of the skin. Zero gravity and water immersion are important environmental variables but poor experimental variables: they reduce the information from more than one sensory system, and they introduce other complications. Zero gravity, for example, removes vestibular cues and reduces tactile-kinaesthetic cues, and also allows the subject to float freely unless restrained. Underwater immersion has some similarities to zero gravity: the diver floats freely, and his tactile-kinaesthetic cues are reduced; but gravity continues to operate on his vestibular and postural systems, his underwater breathing equipment may introduce additional cues, and his visual cues may be reduced or changed.

Comparison of the accuracy of the various cues is further hampered by differences in the type of judgement which the subject is asked to make. Sometimes he is asked about the *postural vertical* (the orientation of his own body), sometimes the *visual vertical* (the appearance of a line at which he is looking), and sometimes about a combination of the two. The subject is sometimes allowed to move freely while making the judgement, and is sometimes strapped to a chair. From a practical viewpoint, the most important type of judgement concerns the postural vertical while free-standing, since this is closely related to the ability to balance. Blind people (or sighted people in the dark) can balance quite well provided they have intact vestibular systems; and vestibular-damaged people can usually balance in the light but tend to fall over in the dark. This seems to show that either visual or vestibular cues are sufficient, when combined with normal tactile-kinaesthetic cues. However, blind or vestibular-damaged people are at a disadvantage in difficult balancing situations; so these two sensory systems must in some way supplement each other. Peripheral vision, for example, may improve a person's performance at static balancing by enabling him to see the outline of his hands and body. However, practice is important; unpractised subjects may perform better blindfold than with partial vision.[2]

The hands and arms can give useful kinaesthetic information when balancing. Murray, for example, describes their use when 'balance-climbing': 'For the next two hundred feet we described a curving course over the slab-sea, cautiously balancing up from one rounded hold to another, rarely if ever finding a notch and never an edge or splinter for grasping fingers. The principal task of one's hands was simply that of maintaining, by sense of touch waist-high on the rock-surface, one's sense of equilibrium.'[3]

When gravity is absent, as it is during the major part of space-flight, there is no gravitational vertical. Astronauts are forced to rely on visual frames of reference, such as the direction of the floor; or on tactile-kinaesthetic cues indicating the direction of the feet. Some astronauts complain that they forget their orientation in the spacecraft when they shut their eyes. They also have difficulty in walking, and in controlling other movements.[1]

Underwater experiments have often been carried out with the aim of simulating zero-gravity in space travel – though the simulation is poor. A more legitimate experimental aim is the measurement of the sensitivity of the vestibular system when visual cues are removed and tactile-kinaesthetic cues much reduced. Unfortunately, experimental techniques have varied so much that there is little agreement on the answer to this question, estimates varying between 4° and 180°. The best controlled experiment of this type was probably that of Nelson:[4] he attached his subjects to a two-axis tilt table under water, and asked them to position themselves in various orientations with respect to gravity. He found a large pitch-forward bias in most positions, and a probable error ranging from 15°–40°. He concluded that vestibular sensitivity was only marginally useful. However, sensitivity of this order could well be useful in distinguishing 'up' from 'down' – an ability of vital importance to divers.

It is not clear which cues are most useful in aiding a swimmer to reach the surface. One of the earliest investigators of this question was William James,[5] who pointed out in 1882 that people with vestibular damage often had difficulty in knowing which way was up when they shut their eyes. However, about half of James' vestibular-damaged subjects claimed to manage adequately: presumably they found the tactile-kinaesthetic cues sufficient. Padden[6] measured the time taken by swimmers to reach the surface after a short submersion on a rotating board, with and without vision. Swimmers with vestibular damage always took longer than normal subjects, and they also took longer blindfold than with vision. Normal subjects, on the other hand, did better when blindfold. These results suggest that orientation while swimming depends mainly on vestibular and postural cues, but that visual cues can help vestibular-damaged swimmers.

A diver wearing breathing apparatus has rather more cues than a swimmer. The breathing valve gives air at different rates as the diver changes his orientation: breathing becomes harder in the inverted position. Exhaust air bubbles float upwards, and can be seen or felt. The air tank and other equipment press against the diver's body, and negatively buoyant objects hang downwards. The diver himself rises and sinks as he inhales and exhales. The face-mask also allows much clearer vision than can be obtained by opening the eyes directly in water; but this is a doubtful advantage unless good visual cues are available.

Experiments on free-swimming divers[7] have shown that they can orient their bodies in an upright or inverted position, with a mean error ranging from 8°–33° depending on the conditions. This was primarily a balancing task, so it is perhaps not surprising that errors were mainly in the pitch-forward direction, and were greater when the diver was upside down (Plate 6). However, Nelson found similar errors in subjects who were attached to a tilt-table and had no difficulties in balancing, so the errors may represent perceptual biasses and uncertainties. It has been suggested[8] that there is a 'vestibular blind-spot' in the inverted position, the vestibular system providing no sensory information. A more likely explanation is that most people have little experience of the inverted position, and have not learned to interpret the available cues accurately.

The role of vision in diver-orientation is obscure. Visual cues to the vertical tend to be meagre in most outdoor diving sites; plants sway in the currents, man-made objects are absent (or lie, like shipwrecks, in non-vertical orientations), and low visibility may obliterate almost all cues. Ross and her colleagues[7] found that, in clear water in the sea, vision helped divers to balance in an inverted position; and helped them to point more accurately to the vertical, whether upright or inverted. This is possibly because vision enabled them to see their bodies, thus helping the kinaesthetic sense in difficult balancing tasks. Restricted vision, on the other hand, may cause worse performance than when blindfold: low-visibility water, or misted facemasks, may be more distracting than dark water, especially to inexperienced divers.

Knowledge of the vertical is certainly poor under water, but most experimental data suggest that a normal diver should be able to reach the surface without difficulty. Nevertheless, divers sometimes report severe disorientation, lasting for about half a minute. These experiences are probably due to pressure vertigo (Ch. 6); or to being swept around in turbulent water; or to adaptation to an off-vertical orientation; or to other types of conflict between the available cues.

II The Apparent Vertical When Cues Conflict

It has been assumed so far that all cues are 'good' cues – potentially helpful, and certainly not misleading. This is not always the case. 'Bad' cues can conflict with 'good' cues, causing a discrepancy between the apparent and true vertical.

The most common source of conflict is between the visual and the vestibular-kinaesthetic vertical. A potential conflict of this sort arises when the eye is tilted, due to head or body tilt, so that the retinal image of a vertical object is no longer 'upright' on the retina. There need be no conflict, of course, provided the brain has adequate vestibular-kinaesthetic information about the orientation of the retina, and can use the information to correct the orientation that the retinal image indicates. In broad daylight the compensating system works well, and the world appears upright even when the head is tilted. In the dark this is no longer the case, and a glowing bar appears tilted when the observer is tilted. The direction of apparent tilt depends on various factors.[1] Possibly body tilt is incorrectly perceived; or possibly the brain fails to compensate correctly for the perceived body tilt. Misperceptions of tilt tend to increase under water[9] – a fact which implies that useful cues from the pressure receptors in the surface of the skin have been lost.

When the body is tilted, the direction of the gravitational force and the orientation of the body no longer coincide. Some equivalent effects can be produced by keeping the body erect, but changing the direction of the apparent gravitational vertical. This happens when an accelerative force is applied to the body in a different direction from the gravitational force. For example, a change in the velocity of linear travel (as in a train) produces a force which tends to fling the passenger forwards or backwards; and rotary movement (as in a merry-go-round) produces a centrifugal force, which tends to fling the passenger away from the centre of rotation. The effective direction of force is called the *gravitoinertial vertical*: it is the 'resultant vector' of the gravitational force and the applied force, varying with the strength and direction of the forces. The vestibular and kinaesthetic sense organs have no means of distinguishing the direction of the gravitoinertial vertical from the gravitational vertical. When there are plenty of good visual cues to the vertical, these tend to dominate; but if the observer watches a vertical glowing line in a dark room, the line will normally appear to tilt in the opposite direction to the tilt of the gravitoinertial vertical. This is known as the *oculogravic illusion* (Fig. 5.1). The illusion can prove troublesome to aircraft pilots, who see the dashboard lights

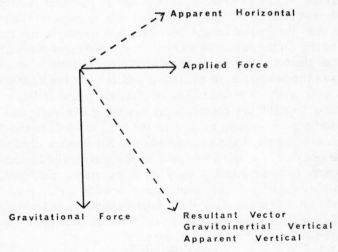

FIGURE 5.1
The oculogravic illusion.

move into a tilted position during certain manœuvres.[1] Skiers, skaters, and other participants in fast sports, also experience large centrifugal forces when turning. They quickly learn to counteract the force by leaning into the turn, balancing in line with the gravitoinertial vertical. They rarely suffer from the oculogravic illusion – perhaps because they actively control their own movement, or perhaps because they are surrounded by strong visual cues to the true vertical.

Sometimes the visual cues are at fault rather than the gravitational cues, as in a tilted room. There is usually some compromise between the conflicting cues, but vision tends to dominate. When the tilted scene fills the whole visual field, it is much more effective than when it fills only part. 'Tilted room' effects are not confined to laboratory experiments. Koffka[10] noted, when travelling up a steep slope in a mountain railway, that the trees seen through the window appeared to grow at an angle to gravity. The Dixons[11] have also commented on the perceptual effects that occur when a stranded yacht lists with the receding tide: the apparent list is less than the true list, and objects known to be vertical (such as an inclinometer) or horizontal (such as the sea) appear correspondingly tilted. Similar effects occur with the *sudden* tilting of ships or planes: the sea or ground appears to tilt much more than the observer's cabin. Repeated experience of sailing[12] or flying[13] reduces the effect, enabling the passenger to rely on gravitational cues (when reliable), or on the visual cues from outside the cabin.

Sometimes the tilted visual cues fill the whole visual scene, and there is no conflict between 'cabin' and 'outside'. This is probably the case with the 'Electric Brae' (Ch. 3), where the whole landscape conspires to give a wrong impression of road tilt. Parker[14] describes a comparable, though unusual, situation when diving: he was working upside down, underneath the hull of a floating ship and the hull formed a natural visual floor. He was positively buoyant, and could 'walk' easily in an inverted position. He quickly accepted this as the upright position – so completely that he wanted to climb 'down' the exit ladder and emerge feet first.

Misleading visual cues can disturb a pilot's sense of the horizontal. For example, when flying in formation he may not know whether the leader has changed attitude or whether he himself has. He may also be misled by the position of the horizon, which is about 4° below the true horizontal when the plane is at 16,000 m. The moon and stars will, quite reasonably, appear to be below the true horizontal. If the pilot attempts to align one wing with the horizon (or false horizontal), the plane will tilt, and the other wing will appear tilted by 8° (instead of by 4° when level).[15]

There is considerable variation in the way people compromise between visual and gravitational cues. Witkin[16] calls those who rely mainly on visual cues 'field dependent', and those who rely on bodily cues 'field independent'. He claims that women and children tend to be more 'field dependent' than men and adults. A more probable explanation is that people learn with experience which cues to rely on in which situations; and men's greater experience of physical skills teaches them to rely on gravitational rather than visual cues.

Experiments on conflicting cues are further complicated by adaptation. A tilted visual scene or a tilted bodily position seems more vertical after a minute or two, and there is a contrasting after-effect when orientation returns to the true vertical.[17] It is often unclear whether the visual or bodily systems adapt, or whether all the systems adapt. The after-effects, however, are quite clear: the runway appears tilted after descending in a tilted plane; and divers who have been in a tilted or inverted orientation report that truly vertical or horizontal objects appear incorrectly orientated.[7, 14]

III   *Learning to Navigate*

Most people have little trouble in knowing which way up they are under normal circumstances; and practice can help them to overcome many of the illusions and uncertainties of strange environments. Navigation is a different matter. People frequently get 'lost', as there are few sensory cues to give them reliable spatial information. They have to use many different sorts of cues to build up a 'cognitive map' of their surroundings, and to know where they are on that map. This ability is of fundamental importance: the blind and the deaf can usually manage to look after themselves, but not those who suffer from spatial confusion. Despite its importance, relatively little is known about the sensory and brain mechanisms involved in spatial cognition.[1]

At first sight, human beings appear to be poorer at navigation than many animals. Some animals possess remarkable abilities to find their way when migrating, or when homing. These abilities are based partly on the recognition of local landmarks, and partly on the innate ability to use certain directional cues.[18] A few animals, such as the European Robin[19] and the American Eel,[20] are sensitive to some aspects of the earth's magnetic field. Many others can use the sun or stars, or polarisation patterns in the blue sky. The general direction for migration is innate in some species, and learned or modifiable in others. One drawback of an innate directional tendency is that it becomes inappropriate if the animal drifts off course and lands in a new locality: a modifiable tendency is a safer mechanism.

Migration is a fairly simple problem: it is necessary only to keep a steady course in one direction at one time of year, and the opposite direction at the other time of year, followed by the recognition of local landmarks at each destination. True navigation, or homing from an unknown place, is much more difficult: the animal has to know approximately where it is in order to go in the right direction. It is not clear how it does this.

Human beings lack a magnetic sense, have no innate ability to use the sun and stars for navigation, and are relatively poor at finding their way home from strange places. However, they have a great capacity for learning, which more than compensates for the lack of innate ability. They have also invented complex and accurate navigational instruments, which may make it unnecessary to rely on primitive cues. Most people acquire elementary navigational skills without much effort, but complex skills require years of training. There are many different types of skilled navigators, such as taxi drivers, climbing guides and ship pilots. Most navigators build up a 'cognitive map' of the area in which they operate, and know the best method of getting from one place to another within that area; they also become experts at dead reckoning, and learn a great variety of directional cues. Modern pilots, however, tend to rely heavily on instruments, and may become lost without them.

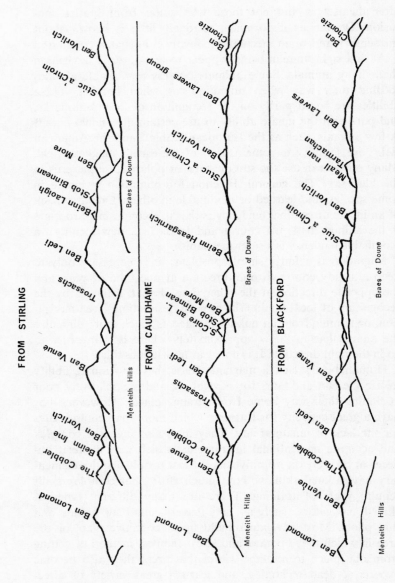

FIGURE 5.2(a) The panorama of Grampian mountains, as seen from three viewpoints.

A large amount of research has been carried out on the development of geographical orientation in children, and on different modes of orientation in adults.[1, 21] Much of this work is concerned with the nature of cognitive maps – whether the maps are orientated to the points of the compass, or centred on the home, or centred on the place where the individual is at

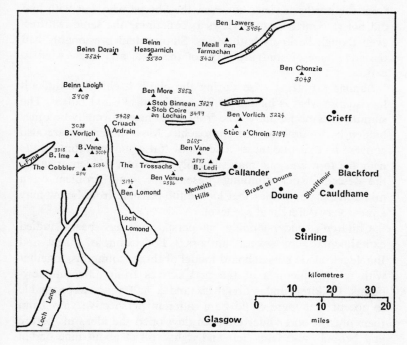

FIGURE 5.2(b)

A map showing the relative positions of the mountains and viewpoints (mountain heights in feet).

present. These differences in cognitive style seem to depend largely on the convention in which one has been trained, and to have little to do with navigational ability.

A more important cognitive skill is the ability to recognise a landscape when viewed from a new angle (Fig. 5.2). The easiest way to understand the relationship of various landmarks is to view them from above – birds and aircraft pilots have a great advantage in this respect. A ground-level view of a mountain range, or the sea-level view of a tortuous coastline, may be quite inadequate for building a three-dimensional image of the area. An example of this is described by Eric Shipton:[22] he was approaching Mount Everest from a new direction, and was able to recognise the peaks and saddles which were familiar to him from the northern view; however, the Sherpa who was with him did not recognize the two views as containing the same features, even though he knew both views. Shipton had presumably had the advantage of studying maps of the area, and knew what to expect.

Similar problems arise during the climb itself – it is difficult to visualise what is hidden by intervening peaks and bulges. The summit of a mountain, visible from a distance, normally becomes hidden by foothills as one approaches. Most mountains are also convex, so that one meets a series of 'false summits' until quite near the top; and one may suddenly encounter hidden crags on the descent. Rock climbing presents the same problem on a miniature scale: routes that look quite possible from below may appear very different at eye level.

Children's understanding of perspective has been studied experimentally by several authors.[21] For example, Piaget and Inhelder[23] made a pasteboard model of three mountains, together with several pictures of the perspectives from different viewpoints. Children under about six and a half years were unable to accept that there could be a different perspective view from their present one. Older children developed the ideas of 'before and behind', and later 'left and right'; till at about nine or ten years they could select the correct view for viewpoints other than their own. However, American six-year-olds can interpret vertical aerial photographs correctly.[24]

IV Orientation to the Points of the Compass

The most reliable guides to the points of the compass are the sun, moon and stars. The use of these cues is not instinctive, but can be learnt with little trouble. Most people know that the sun is in the east at about 6.0 a.m., in the south at about 12.0

noon, and in the west at about 6.0 p.m. For greater accuracy it is necessary to know the latitude and the time of year, and to consult a suitable set of tables.[25, 26] For ordinary navigational purposes a low degree of accuracy may be quite acceptable, since the traveller uses many other cues to guide his journey.

The moon is more complicated to use than the sun, as it rises and sets fifty minutes later each night. However, the illuminated part of its surface always points towards the sun, even when the latter is below the horizon; so it is always possible to take a bearing from the assumed position of the sun at the relevant time of night. The behaviour of the moon may be complicated, but it was not beyond the wit of primitive men to build megalithic observatories which could determine the calendar by their alignment with the moon.[27]

The stars are a simpler guide than the moon, since they can be used independently of time or season to locate the celestial Poles. People all over the world recognise much the same groups of stars, though they give the same constellations different names. The Great Bear or Plough is known as the Dipper in North America; and Orion's belt and sword are known to the Zulus as three pigs pursued by three dogs, and to the Masai as three bachelors pursued by three old maids.[28] However, some cultures, such as the Aranda of South Australia, employ different groupings.[29] Regardless of names and groupings, most people know that the constellations rise in the east and set in the west, appearing to revolve anti-clockwise around the celestial North Pole, and clockwise around the celestial South Pole. Stars reach the same position in the sky four minutes earlier each night; and given sufficient charts, or a good memory,[30] it is possible to know the bearing of any star at any date, time and place.

In tropical countries the constellations near the Poles are hard to see; but the zodiacal constellations (such as Orion) give good easterly points when rising and westerly points when setting. From the equator, stars appear to rise and set vertically, so that it is easy to determine east and west quite accurately. The navigators of Puluwat (Caroline Islands) use the rising and setting stars to define thirty-two points of the compass.[31] They regard east as the cardinal direction, lying under the rising of the 'Big Bird' – Altair, a bright star in Aquila ('The Eagle'). The thirty-two points are not equally spaced, so do not coincide exactly with the mariner's compass. This does not matter, since the Puluwat navigators learn the appropriate 'star courses' between pairs of islands.

There are all sorts of other cues which can be used as rough compass bearings.[25, 26, 28] The prevailing wind produces certain patterns of sand or snow dunes, and bends the trees and shrubs. The snow in north-facing corries lasts far into the summer in high mountains; and rocks and trees produce characteristic melt-shadows or melt-holes in the snow. Moss tends to grow on the dampest and darkest side of trees and rocks. Buildings in cool climates generally face the sun, while those in hot climates face away from the sun. Churches are often orientated in an east–west direction, with the altar to the rising sun. The yellow ants of the Alps build oblong anthills, orientated rather like churches, with the highest point and steepest side facing south-east, to catch the warmth of the winter sun. There are many other small cues of this sort, which the observant traveller quickly learns.

V   Travelling in a Straight Line

It is often unimportant to know one's compass bearing, provided one can keep travelling in a straight line. The cues mentioned in the previous section can all be used to pursue a straight path, given time-compensation for celestial bodies over long journeys. Travellers may also make use of sounds and smells; and they may recognise different types of winds, and notice when they change direction.

Winds and waves are particularly important at sea. The Puluwat navigators use the waves not only to steer a steady course, but partly as a compass, since they can distinguish the waves coming from different directions.[31] Orientation to the waves is achieved by a sense of motion, rather than by vision. The motion pattern for head-on and broadside waves are quite distinguishable, the former causing pitch and the latter roll. Any deviation from a perpendicular orientation causes a slight roll, and any deviation from parallel introduces some pitch. When diagonal to the waves, both pitch and roll are marked, and small changes in orientation are hard to detect.

The most direct route may not always be the easiest way of reaching one's destination. Paths are generally better because they remove uncertainty and avoid obstacles. Arab guides in the Sahara desert may rely on faint winding trails rather than head straight for a visible destination, since storms and mirages can make the latter unreliable.[32] In dense forests the destination is invisible: foresters mark the trees as signposts, or learn the larger paths made by animals. Hill walkers mark their routes with cairns; and divers, who frequently operate in limited visibility, with ropes.

Once a mist descends, the poverty of man's directional sense becomes obvious. In the absence of visual cues, people tend to veer or circle. The bodily cues – presumably based on the tactile, kinaesthetic or vestibular senses – are inadequate to detect small changes of direction; a slight bias in the sensory system is sufficient to produce veering over a short distance. This is particularly serious under water: divers have been known to drown when surfacing underneath a large flat-bottomed boat, being unable to swim straight to one side of it.

Most investigators claim that people veer to the right rather than the left, particularly when on foot.[1] Schaeffer[33] claimed that swimmers were different, tending to veer left. People certainly veer more when swimming than walking[34] but the direction is unclear. One theory of veering is that it is due to asymmetrical limb length, or asymmetrical muscular strength. Lund[35] for example, claimed that the left leg is about 5 mm longer than the right, and that this accounts for the tendency to veer right. However, it could equally well be argued that a stronger right leg should cause veering to the left. Moreover, it is hard to see how bodily asymmetry could cause veering when driving a car, or account for variation in the direction of veering in the same individual. The cause of veering is probably not any structural asymmetry, but some imbalance in the vestibular or kinaesthetic systems. Schaeffer proposed that there was an 'innate spiralling mechanism' which takes over in the absence of other sensory control, and is similar to the autokinetic effect (Ch. 6). He pointed out that blindfold passengers on a train or boat may feel that the vehicle is following a curved path when it is actually going straight. Similarly, divers sometimes report a feeling of curvature when following a straight rope.[34] Larger sensations of apparent veering on a straight path can, of course, be induced as an after-effect of following a curved path;[36] in such cases it is quite clear that adaptation of some directional sense is the cause, rather than bodily asymmetries. It seems probable that veering tendencies and curvature after-effects have a similar origin, though the precise nature of the sensory mechanisms is obscure.

VI   Dead Reckoning and Homing

Dead reckoning depends on estimating the distance and direction travelled since the last known location. One is lost if one loses track of either of these, unless one meets another familiar landmark. Though primitive, the method can be more useful than a map and compass: for example, when lost in a mist one may not be able to locate oneself on the map, and may not know which compass bearing one should take. In such circumstances one has to rely, consciously or unconsciously, on dead reckoning.

Successful navigation by dead reckoning involves three stages: (1) setting out in the appropriate direction; (2) holding a steady course, keeping a running estimate of position, and checking expected landmarks along the way; (3) locating the destination and homing in on it. The problems of directional navigation have already been mentioned; but the problem of distance raises further questions of time and speed. The apparent distance travelled is distorted by any factors which alter the apparent speed of travel or the apparent time taken for the journey: a decrease in apparent speed or an increase in apparent time makes the distance seem longer. Real changes in speed or time have similar effects, presumably because people miscalculate at least one of the factors. Thus a distance seems longer when walked rather than run.[37] It may also seem longer if great effort is involved, or if the route is new, or if the traveller is tired or anxious. However, this subject is as confused and contradictory

as that of time perception (Ch. 2), and it is easy to cite conflicting cases. For example, Galton[26] claims that journeys seem
longer when the traveller is fresh, because the alert mind notices
more details and thus prolongs the apparent time; whereas
many people would claim that tiredness makes journeys longer.
MacInnes[38] claims that most people under-estimate time and
distance, once out on the hills; but Gatty[25] maintains that they
over-estimate distances.

Experimental evidence is meagre, and often confusing. One
source of confusion is the difference between the methods of
reproduction and *estimation*: in the former method the subject
attempts to travel a named distance, while in the latter he
attempts to estimate verbally a distance which he has covered.
Logically, the two methods should give equivalent results, with
over-estimation in one method meaning the same as under-
estimation in the other. Psychologically, the methods may not
be the same: estimating a distance which one has followed is
not the same as striking out into the unknown for a given
distance. For example, people may over-estimate the distance
they have covered in a mist, yet also walk too far when asked
to reproduce a given distance. Blindfold divers, especially
novices, tend to swim too far when asked to reproduce short
distances;[34] but they tend to stop short when reproducing longer
distances, particularly when attempting to swim down to a given
depth.[39] This is probably due to a quite reasonable fear of
going too deep, or too far for safety. Similarly, blindfold subjects stop short when pacing out distances near a precipitous
drop![40]

Navigators do not always travel in a straight line. Sometimes
they make deliberate angular errors to ensure that when they
meet a road or river they will know whether to follow it to the
left or right to meet a landmark. Navigation of this sort involves
the ability to judge angles; but there seems to be little direct
experimental evidence on angular errors during bodily turns.
Triangle-completion tests – the ability to return to the starting
post when blindfold, after following two sides of a triangle –
give ambiguous results because both angular and distance errors
may be involved. It seems likely that kinaesthetic cues are more
important than vestibular cues in this type of judgement, since

vestibular-defective subjects perform as well as normal subjects,[41] and because performance is poorer under water than on land.[34]

The Caroline Islanders use a system known as *etak*[31] or *hatag*[42] to help them navigate during their sea journeys. They measure the distance they have covered by noting the changed bearing of a reference island in relation to the stars (Fig. 5.3). They select a suitable reference island to one side of the route,

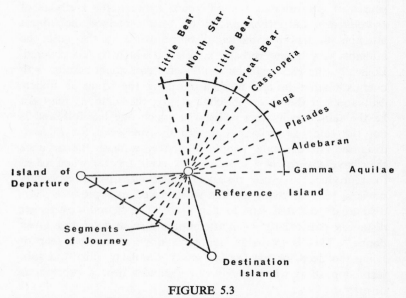

FIGURE 5.3

The principle of *etak*. (After T. Gladwin, *East is a Big Bird*, Cambridge, Mass.: Harvard University Press, 1970.)

which divides the journey into approximately equal segments (usually about ten miles long) as it appears to pass each 'navigation star position'. Towards the end of the journey the navigator homes in on the island by noticing signs, such as the patterns of the waves, or the flight of birds returning to land at dusk. Fishermen off our own islands sometimes make similar use of bird flight when lost in a mist: the inhabitants of St Kilda in 1750 preferred this method to a compass.[43]

VII   *Navigation in a City*

Navigation in a city is a very different problem from navigation at sea or in the hills. Paths and landmarks are more important, and the points of the compass less relevant. However, there is one similarity between navigation at sea and travel in a large city: both are dynamic.[31] Wind and currents at sea, and traffic patterns in a city, are liable to change at short notice. The skilled taxi driver knows the times and locations of one-way streets and traffic jams; and he learns the best way of driving between two places in different circumstances. Pedestrians learn slightly different rules: they can walk through one-way streets, but any navigational error is likely to be much more expensive in time and effort than it is for a car driver. Travel by public transport is different again: it is unnecessary to know the details of the route, provided one knows where to board and leave vehicles, and the best times of day to wait for transport.

Some cities have more 'imageability' than others. Lynch[44] points out that some are featureless, while others are divided into recognisable areas with good landmarks. However, the possession of distinctive features is not sufficient to ensure that people will acquire a correct cognitive map of the city. For example, Boston (Massachussetts) is high on 'imageability'; but it contains a five-sided common which people suppose to be a square, leading to misconceptions of the orientation of surrounding roads and landmarks. Triangles and curved roads also cause difficulties. 'Three-dimensional' cities, with bridges and underpasses and 'spaghetti junctions', strike some motorists with confusion and terror.

Incorrect cognitive maps are sometimes developed accidentally during the first visit to a city, and are then very difficult to rectify. On subsequent visits people may become disorientated and believe that everything is the wrong way round.[45, 46] Misleading sketch-maps can also cause trouble. For example, the London Underground Railway provides highly schematic maps of the routes: these are quite adequate as instructions for the order of the stations, and for the intersections with other lines;

but they are very misleading as a guide to the true relations between the stations.

Misperceptions of distance in a city can arise among its citizens, even when they have ample opportunity to see correct maps and to learn of their mistakes. Indeed, some of the mistakes probably develop through familiarity: the citizens generally imagine the city centre to be larger, and the outskirts smaller, than reality. Fisher[47] has produced 'perceptual maps' of Newcastle and other towns, based on the reports of the inhabitants and showing the supposed relationships of the main roads and landmarks. Whether such a map would be a help or a hindrance to either a newcomer or a seasoned citizen is a moot point.

The apparent expansion or contraction of different parts of a city is a pliable phenomenon: it may well depend on what questions are asked, and which places are compared. Some methods seem to show expansion of the city centre, others the opposite. For example, Lee[48] found that journeys towards the centre were judged shorter than different journeys of the same distance in the out-of-town direction. The shopping behaviour of women is consistent with this finding: they prefer to use shops in the direction of the town centre, rather than nearer shops away from town.[49] There may, of course, be several reasons why women prefer to go into town; but it may well be true that a familiar journey seems short, particularly when the destination is desirable. This is not necessarily incompatible with the apparent expansion of the central area, which is filled with interesting landmarks. Perceptual judgements of time and distance rarely show the symmetry and logical consistency desired of them by experimental psychologists.

The blind can become expert at following familiar routes through a city, but have great difficulty with new routes. They cannot see landmarks which would be obvious to a sighted person, and must rely on objects that they will meet and touch. If they are following a route map, they must stay on route or they will get lost. Maps for the blind must be based on the main cues that the blind use, such as the kerbs at the end of each street block. Leonard and Newman[50] devised three kinds of maps for the blind. One of these is a disc divided into segments corresponding to street blocks, each with a simple braille code giving instructions such as 'turn left'. The disc has a cursor which can be moved after each block, to remind the traveller where he is in the instructions. A second type of 'map' is a portable tape-recorder, with verbal instructions about each section. The third type, and perhaps the most versatile, is a raised route diagram, or a tactile model, in which the correct side of the road is indicated by raised or roughened material. There are, of course, many mechanical and electronic devices which help the blind to detect obstacles and navigate on a very small scale;[51] but large-scale navigation demands some type of 'map', which gives information and instructions about objects further afield.

This chapter has considered various aspects of orientation out of doors. Much of the material is unsatisfactory: 'facts' are contradictory or non-existent; 'theories' inadequate or untestable. Some readers will find this state of affairs intriguing and challenging; others will pass on with relief to a topic which has been minutely and extensively studied – movement perception.

NOTES

1 A more detailed discussion can be found in I. P. Howard and W. B. Templeton, *Human Spatial Orientation*, London: Wiley, 1966.

2 J. Dickinson and J. A. Leonard, 'The role of peripheral vision in static balancing', *Ergonomics*, 1967, Vol. 10, pp. 421–9.

3 W. H. Murray, *Mountaineering in Scotland*, London: Dent, 1947, p. 50.

4 J. G. Nelson, 'The effect of water immersion and body position upon perception of the gravitational vertical', *Aerospace Med.*, 1968, Vol. 39, pp. 806–11.

5 W. James, 'The sense of dizziness in deaf-mutes', *Amer. J. Otol.*, 1882, Vol. 4, pp. 239–54.

6 D. A. Padden, 'Ability of deaf swimmers to orient themselves when submerged in water', *Res. Quart. Amer. Ass. Hlth. Phys. Educ. Rec.*, 1959, Vol. 30, pp. 214–26.

7 H. E. Ross, S. D. Crickmar, N. V. Sills and E. P. Owen, 'Orientation to the vertical in free divers', *Aerospace Med.*, 1969, Vol. 40, pp. 728–32.

8 F. H. Quix, 'Un nouvel appareil pour l'examen du nystagmus de position', *J. Neurol., Brux.*, 1928, Vol. 3, pp. 160–80.

9 C. Sziklai, *Underwater studies of space orientation*. Ph.D. Thesis, Clark University, 1966.

10 K. Koffka, *Principles of Gestalt Psychology*, London: Routledge & Kegan Paul, 1935, p. 216.
11 N. F. Dixon and P. M. Dixon, ' "Sloping water" and related framework illusions: some informal observations', *Q.J. exp. Psychol.*, 1966, Vol. 18, pp. 369–70.
12 H. von Helmholtz, *Treatise on physiological optics*, Vol. 3, p. 250, New York: Dover 1962.
13 S. H. Bartley, *Perception in Everyday Life*, New York: Harper & Row, 1972, p. 39.
14 G. Parker, 'Think deep', *Skin Diver*, September 1969, pp. 22–3, 56.
15 A. J. Benson, 'Spatial disorientation in flight', Ch. 40 in *'A Textbook of Aviation Physiology'*, edited by J. A. Gillies, Oxford: Pergamon, 1965.
16 H. A. Witkin, 'The perception of the upright', *Scientific American*, 1959, Vol. 200, pp. 50–6.
17 N. J. Wade, 'Effect of prolonged tilt on visual orientation', *Q.J. exp. Psychol.*, 1970, Vol. 22, pp. 423–39.
18 For reviews of animal navigation, see I. Eibl-Eibesfeldt, *Ethology: the biology of behavior* (translated by E. Klinghammer), New York: Holt, Rinehart & Winston, 1970 (Ch. 16); and R. A. Hinde, *Animal Behavior: a synthesis of ethology and comparative psychology*, New York: McGraw-Hill, 1970 (Ch. 7).
19 W. Wiltschke and R. Wiltschke, 'Magnetic compass of European Robins', *Science*, 1972, Vol. 176, pp. 62–4.
20 S. A. Rommel Jr. and J. D. McCleave, 'Oceanic electric fields: Perception by American Eels?', *Science*, 1972, Vol. 176, pp. 1233–5.
21 R. A. Hart and G. T. Moore, 'The development of spatial cognition: a review', in *Image and environment: cognitive mapping and spatial behavior*, edited by R. M. Downs and D. Stea, Chicago: Aldine-Atherton, 1973.
22 E. E. Shipton, *The Mount Everest Reconnaisance Expedition*, London: Hodder & Stoughton, 1952.
23 J. Piaget and B. Inhelder, *The Child's Conception of Space*, New York: Norton, 1967.
24 J. M. Blaut, G. F. McCleary and A. S. Blaut, 'Environmental mapping in young children', *Environment and Behavior*, 1970, Vol. 2, pp. 335–49.
25 H. Gatty, *Nature is Your Guide*, London: Collins, 1958.
26 F. Galton, *The Art of Travel; or, shifts and contrivances available in wild countries* (London: Murray, 1872), reprinted by David & Charles, Newton Abbot, 1971.
27 A. Thom, *Megalithic Lunar Observations*, Oxford: Clarendon, 1971.
28 R. S. S. Baden-Powell, *Scouting for Boys*, London: Pearson, 1944.
29 B. G. Maegraith, 'The astronomy of the Aranda and Luritja tribes', *Transactions of the Royal Society of South Australia*, 1932, Vol. 56, No. 10.
30 To illustrate that no great strain need be placed on the memory, the following mnemonic shows how the orientation of the Pointers of the Plough can be used to obtain the time:

We picture on the Northern sky a twelve-hour clock-dial, vast
and high,
And for its central point in space the steadfast North Star holds
the place.
'Tis mid-October, and we fix the Pointers' hand at figure six.
The number of the month and hour we double now, which gives
us power
To wrest from 'forty-one and half' the time of night.
With merry laugh we hear, along the homing line, the church
bells chiming half-past nine.

(Solution: Double month $(2 \times 10 = 20)$ plus doubled hour
$(2 \times 6 = 12)$ is 32. Subtract 32 from $41\frac{1}{2}$, and the answer $(9\frac{1}{2})$ is
9.30 p.m.).
This mnemonic appears in an undated booklet by F. W. Murray,
Astronomy Simply Explained for Beginners, Glasgow: Brown, Son
& Ferguson, p. 19.

31   T. Gladwin, *East is a Big Bird* (*navigation and logic on Puluwat
     Atoll*), Cambridge, Mass.: Harvard University Press, 1970.
32   P. Jaccard, *Le sens de la direction et l'orientation lointaine chez
     l'homme*, Paris: Payot, 1932.
33   A. A. Schaeffer, 'Spiral movement in man', *J. Morphology*, 1928,
     Vol. 45, pp. 293–398.
34   H. E. Ross, D. J. Dickinson and B. P. Jupp, 'Geographical orienta-
     tion under water', *Human Factors*, 1970, Vol. 12, pp. 13–23.
35   F. H. Lund, 'Physical asymmetries and disorientation', *Amer. J.
     Psychol.*, 1930, Vol. 42, 51–62.
36   B. J. Cratty, 'Perceptual alterations of veer by interpolated move-
     ment experience', *Research Quarterly*, 1965, Vol. 36, pp. 22–28.
37   J. Cohen, P. Cooper and A. Ono, 'The hare and the tortoise: a
     study of the *tau*-effect in walking and running', *Acta Psychol.*,
     1963, Vol. 21, pp. 387–93.
38   H. MacInnes, *Climbing*, Edinburgh: Scottish Youth Hostels Asso-
     ciation, 1963, p. 11.
39   H. E. Ross and S. S. Franklin, 'Depth estimation in divers', in
     Progress in Underwater Science, edited by J. N. Lythgoe, London:
     Academic Press, 1974.
40   H. Werner and S. Wapner, 'Changes in psychological distance under
     conditions of danger', *J. Personality*, 1954, Vol. 24, pp. 153–67.
41   P. Worchel, 'The role of vestibular organs in space orientation',
     J. exp. Psychol., 1952, Vol. 44, pp. 4–10.
42   W. H. Alkire, 'Systems of measurement on Woleai Atoll, Caroline
     Islands', *Anthropos*, 1970, Vol. 65.
43   M. Martin, *A Voyage to St. Kilda* (1753), Edinburgh: James Thin,
     1970, p. 7.
44   K. Lynch, *The Image of the City*, Cambridge, Mass.: M.I.T. Press,
     1960.
45   M. A. Binet, 'Reverse illusions of orientation', *Psychol. Rev.*, 1894,
     Vol. 1, pp. 337–50.
46   J. Peterson, 'Illusions of direction orientation', *J. Phil. Psych. Sci.
     Meth.*, 1916, Vol. 13, pp. 225–36.
47   G. H. Fisher, *The Perceptual Map of Newcastle upon Tyne*,

Department of Psychology, University of Newcastle upon Tyne, 1971.

48 T. R. Lee, 'Perceived distance as a function of direction in the city', *Environment and Behavior*, 1970, Vol. 2, pp. 40–51.

49 T. R. Lee, '"Brennan's Law" of shopping behavior', *Psychol. Rep.*, 1962, Vol. 11, p. 662.

50 J. A. Leonard and R. C. Newman, 'Three types of "maps" for blind travel', *Ergonomics*, 1970, Vol. 13, pp. 165–79.

51 R. Dufton (Ed.), *Proceedings of the International Conference on Sensory Devices for the Blind*, London: St. Dunstan's, 1967.

CHAPTER 6

The Perception of Movement

Movement is a relative matter; when an object moves, it must move in relation to some other object. The observer is always faced with the difficulty of deciding which of two objects moved, or whether both moved, or whether his own eyes or body moved. Usually his brain sorts this out quickly and accurately, and he perceives the true source of movement. Sometimes the visual or bodily information is misleading, and he then suffers an illusion. This is particularly likely to happen in novel surroundings, or with fast methods of transport for which the human body was not designed. This chapter starts by considering illusions which are mainly visual, and then proceeds to those which stem mainly from unusual bodily stimulation.

I   *The After-effect of Visual Movement*

Most readers will have noticed the after-effect that arises from staring at a moving pattern, and then looking at a stationary surface: the surface appears to move slowly in the opposite direction to the previous real movement. This effect was reported in antiquity by Aristotle and Lucretius, and by several early psychologists.[1] Purkinje[2] noticed it after watching a military parade, in about 1823. One of the best-known descriptions was given by a chemist, Addams, in 1834. He was on holiday in the Scottish Highlands, and went to admire the Falls of Foyers on the border of Loch Ness. He stared at the waterfall at eye level for some seconds, and then happened to glance at the rock face to the left of the fall: 'I saw the rocky surface as if in motion upwards, and with an apparent velocity equal to that of the descending water, which the moment before had prepared my eyes to behold this singular deception.'[3] Sylvanus P. Thompson, a physicist, took his holidays near the Rhine, and noticed that if one first fixated the fast-flowing water in midstream for some time, and then transferred one's gaze to the slower water near the bank, the slow water appeared to flow backwards. Thompson noticed an amusing variant on this while travelling in a train: if one stares in the direction of travel, objects approach and expand, and if one then looks at stationary objects they appear to recede and contract. The reverse happens after watching retreating objects . . . 'The effect is more amusing if, after observing either of these cases of motion, we transfer our gaze to the face of a fellow-passenger sitting opposite.'[4]

Addams thought the after-effect was due to involuntary and unconscious eye-movements in the same direction as the real movement, which continued after the real movement had stopped. He assumed that the brain would fail to make any allowance for such eye-movements, and would interpret the retinal image movement as real movement. However, Thompson pointed out that the movement after-effect from a rotating object occurs in all directions at once, so cannot be due to eye-movements. He suggested instead that areas of the retina which are constantly stimulated by movement in any one direction become 'fatigued', so that relatively little motion is perceived; and when the real motion stops, the contrasting sensation in that region of the retina is interpreted as movement in the opposite direction.[5] This type of explanation is basically similar to modern neuro-physiological findings; cells in the retina or brain which are sensitive to movement in a particular direction adapt to constant stimulation and reduce their rate of firing. The difference in firing rate between cells of opposite directional-sensitivity can account for the perceived direction of movement.[6]

II *Induced Movement*

A popular device at fairgrounds in the last century was the 'haunted swing':[7] artificial scenery swung to and fro outside the cabin window would make the stationary occupants feel as though they were rocking. Modern fairs use more expensive machinery to amuse people, but 'induced movement' can still be observed freely in everyday life. A common example is the experience of sitting in a stationary train and watching another train move past the window: one tends to perceive one's own train as moving and the other train as stationary.[4] Similarly, when a visual scene moves rapidly across a television screen, one may see the frame as moving and the picture as stationary. *Relative* movement is correctly perceived, but some of the movement is wrongly ascribed to the foreground or framework rather than to the background. These effects have been well known for centuries, but were first investigated in the laboratory by Duncker in the 1920s.[2]

Induced movement can occur without the intervention of machinery. The clouds racing past in the sky can induce movement in the moon, stars or sun; and they can make tall buildings and mountains appear to topple over. It was probably cloud movement which caused Murray to experience the following phenomenon: 'After two hours of uphill tramping in sultry air I felt released in a world lively and free, which awakened in me the illusion of watching the spin of the earth and its flight through interstellar space. This sensation sprang from both sight and touch: the brush of the wind on my cheek, the lift of the moon, the glide of some wisps of cirrus, and more especially of the stars, which seemed to race behind them . . . The illusion lasted half a minute and disappeared with the arrival of Mackinnon.'[8]

It has sometimes been suggested that induced movement is due to unconscious eye-movements, which the brain fails to take into account. However, there is no correlation between the direction of eye movements and of apparent movement.[9] The illusion seems to be due to the brain's assumption that the main part of the visual field is less likely to be moving than smaller parts. Normally this is a reasonable assumption, but sometimes it leads to errors.

III *The Autokinetic Effect*

In the 1850s it was reported by the astronomer Von Humboldt, and by various others,[2] that stars sometimes appeared to move around. This effect was termed 'autokinetic' (self-moving) by Aubert in 1887. After staring at a dim light in the dark for a few seconds, the light may appear to move of its own accord. The effect does not disappear with practice, but can be avoided by moving the eyes frequently. It can be quite dangerous to aircraft pilots, who sometimes crash because they mistake stars or ground lights for the lights of moving planes.[10]

Mountaineers sometimes report the apparent movement of rocks on the skyline, particularly in a mist. This makes the rocks look like climbers. The possibility of this illusion adds to the controversy as to whether Mallory and Irvine could have reached the summit of Mount Everest in 1924.[11] Odell claimed to have seen them on the 'second rock step', about 260 m below the summit, and to have watched them climbing for a few minutes during a break in the mist. Others have doubted whether the time and place of the sighting were at all likely. Shipton and Smythe had a similar experience at about the same place on the 1933 expedition. Shipton looked up and said, 'There go Wyn and Waggers on the second step.' Smythe saw the same thing: '. . . Sure enough, there were two little dots on a steep snow-slope at the foot of the cliff. We stared hard at them and could have sworn they moved. Then, simultaneously, we realized that they were rocks. And, strangely enough, there are two more rocks perched on a snow-slope immediately above the step; these again looked like men and appeared to move when stared at.'[12]

Murray describes a similar incident in the Cairngorms: 'When we started on the last rise to Cairn Toul there came a wider clearance than usual. Suddenly Mortimer gripped my arm and pointed uphill through the misty chasm. "Look!" he exclaimed, "Two men crossing to Glen Einich." Upon looking up at the slope I was duly surprised to see two climbers a long way ahead of us . . . I watched them traverse a full fifty feet from east to west across the snow-slope, one about ten yards in front of the other . . . We advanced and saw them halt, apparently to wait for us. At a hundred yards' range they turned out to be two black boulders. So great was our astonishment that we failed even to laugh at ourselves. It was a perfect illustration of the eye's absolute need of some framework before it can distinguish a moving object from a stationary.'[8]

The absence of a framework is unlikely to be the full explanation of the autokinetic effect, though it is a necessary condition for its occurrence. Suggestions by other people can be important,[2] as illustrated in the mountaineering examples. The effect is probably not due to eye-movements, since it can occur when the eyes are still. It may be due to a minor imbalance in the muscular control of the position of the neck or eyes, with the result that there is a change in the felt position of the eyes. Since there is no real change in their position, the brain interprets the spot of light as moving.[13]

IV Reversed Rotation

Reversed rotary movement – or the 'kinetic depth effect' – has been reported by many writers, one of the earliest being Robert Smith in 1738.[1] The effect is likely to occur in the twilight when viewing ambiguous objects, such as a windmill or a crow on the skyline: the windmill may appear to oscillate, or rotate in the wrong direction; and the crow may appear to have one revolving wing instead of one near wing flapping up and down.

The cause of the illusion is that there is very little difference in the pattern of change of the retinal image for clockwise and counter-clockwise rotation, and with distant objects it may be impossible to tell which is the back and which the front. If the true back and front are apparently reversed, the movement will appear to go in the wrong direction. Reversal sometimes occurs with close objects, if they are viewed in poor light with one eye: a wire model of a cube can give rise to the effect. Such a cube may appear back to front even when it is touched;[14] and it will then appear to rotate in the wrong direction if either the cube or the observer's head is moved.

Lights at night can appear to move when stationary, or to rotate in the wrong direction, when the apparent distances of the lights are misinterpreted. This is probably the cause of some road and air accidents.[10] Reversal is most likely to occur when the lights at the back are larger or brighter than those at the front, because the brain assumes that they are the same size but nearer.

Non-rectangular objects are particularly liable to reverse, for

I

the same reason. If the object tapers, as does Ames' 'trapezoidal window',[15] the smaller part will appear behind: reversed motion, oscillation, or true motion will be seen, depending on the relative retinal sizes of the true front and back. Ames believed that familiarity with rectanglar objects was important in producing oscillation. Some support for this point of view was provided by Allport and Pettigrew,[16] who found that country-dwelling Zulus (who lived in a 'round' environment) were not quite as susceptible to the effect as town-dwellers (who lived in a 'carpentered' environment). However, the differences between the two groups were very slight, and appeared only under close viewing conditions. In fact, it seems that reversals are likely to be seen whenever the visual depth information conflicts with the true depth, whether the object is familiar to the viewer or not.[17]

Commonsense would suggest that familiarity with the true shape of the object would make one slightly *less* susceptible to illusions of reversed motion. The illusion is unstable, and can sometimes be abolished by 'will-power'; so pilots probably make fewer mistakes about the meaning of runway lights at night if they are familiar with the layout of the airport by day.

V *Stroboscopic Movement*

'Stroboscopic movement' or the 'phi phenomenon' is another illusion caused mainly by the visual stimulus: if two flashes of light follow each other closely enough in time and space, they appear as one moving light rather than two separate lights. The earliest experiments were performed by Exner[2] in 1875, and the effect is frequently used nowadays in illuminated signs and advertisements. Some authors argue that there are important differences between phi movement and real movement,[18] but most maintain that they are the same thing:[19] discrete flashes of light at the correct spatial and temporal intervals provide almost the same retinal stimulus as real movement, and are naturally mistaken for it. As with most types of movement perception, the effect depends on a change of *apparent* location rather than *retinal* location – any eye movements are taken into account.[20]

Movement illusions can also occur when truly moving objects are illuminated intermittently (stroboscopically). If the flash interval is correct, the retinal stimulation can be the same as that of an object moving in the opposite direction. Trick effects of this sort are sometimes produced at fairgrounds: drops of water can apparently flow upwards, and wheels run backwards. The same thing may happen in old films with relatively few frames a second. This stroboscopic effect is unusual in nature; but wheels may appear distorted or seem to run backwards when viewed through railings or fences, due to shifting moiré patterns.[21]

A mild stroboscopic effect can occur naturally when driving down a road in bright sunlight, shaded by regular trees or fences. The rhythmic alternation between light and shadow is very annoying, and can cause dizziness and nausea. If there is a steady flicker at ten to fifteen flashes per second, susceptible people may suffer an epileptic fit. This is more likely to happen at a discotheque, where stroboscopic lights are deliberately used to produce various perceptual and sensory effects.

Movement often appears jerky under intermittent illumination. The jerkiness depends on various factors such as the flash rate, the brightness of the object, and whether the viewer is fixating the object or its background. Some of these effects can be noticed in front of a television screen. At a normal viewing distance, the flicker on the screen is not noticeable; but if a hand is moved in front of the screen, the hand movement appears jerky. If the hand is fixated instead of the screen, the hand movement appears smooth and the television screen appears to flicker. A self-illuminated object, such as a glowing cigarette end, is of course visible continuously: it will move steadily under strobo-scopic light, and appear to become dissociated from the small jerky movements of the unlit portion.

Raindrops and snowflakes fall in discrete units, but sometimes appear as streaks. This is because the *critical flicker frequency* (the speed at which flicker vanishes and continuity is seen) depends on the brightness contrast and the on/off ratio of the retinal stimulus. Raindrops fall fast, and normally appear as streaks. Snowflakes fall more slowly, and have higher brightness contrast than raindrops; the nearby flakes have a higher retinal speed than further flakes, and may appear to form white cords, while the further flakes appear as units.

Some rain and snow effects are not primarily due to flicker patterns on the retina. For example, snow may appear to float upwards when seen in the headlights of a car, or when looking down from the window of a tall building; this is probably because tall buildings and moving cars can produce eddy currents which are sufficiently powerful to suck snowflakes upwards. Raindrops are too heavy to be much affected by such currents. Rain normally falls vertically, unless a strong wind blows it obliquely. Nevertheless, when travelling in a car or train, vertical rain seen from a side window appears to fall obliquely against the direction of travel. This is part of the flow-pattern of the visual scene when travelling (Section VIII) – the direction of slant appears to reverse if one looks backwards, or views the rain against a train travelling in the opposite direction.[4]

VI   Size, Distance and Apparent Speed

The visual illusions mentioned so far have been concerned more with changes of apparent direction than with changes of apparent speed. Some other visual illusions are primarily concerned with speed. Apparent speed is normally determined by the apparent distance traversed during a certain apparent time; though in some illusions (particularly the movement after-effect and the autokinetic effect) speed and distance may become divorced, with objects apparently moving and yet not changing their location.

The rate at which the image of a moving object crosses the retina varies at different viewing distances: it is slower at far than near distances, since it traverses a smaller retinal area in the same time. If size-constancy were perfect, the image would cover the same apparent area at all distances, and the result would be perfect speed-constancy. In practice, apparent size and apparent speed decrease together in the distance, speed-constancy being closely related to size-constancy.[22] A change of retinal speed can be a cue to distance, faster speed indicating a nearer distance. This effect is particularly important when watching lights glowing in the dark. A related effect[23] is that slower lights appear larger than faster lights, if they are actually at the same distance and of the same size. Similarly, large lights appear to move more slowly than small lights, when the true distance and speed are the same. Obviously apparent size, distance and speed are related in a predictable manner.

Another waterfall-watching physicist, J. H. Fremlin, recently observed a natural example of the speed-distance effect. Fremlin was gazing at the water running down the spillway of the large dam at Cow Green, in Upper Teesdale. The main flow of water formed a continuous sheet, but the wind was blowing small waves over the dam, which formed faster jets of water on top of the main sheet. As he watched, the faster jets began to appear nearer, standing out in depth like 'moving icicles', or like 'the overlapping ruffled feathers of an angry cock'.[24]

Foggy weather can also produce distortions of apparent speed, since it increases the apparent distance travelled. When first sighted, objects may appear to be at more than twice their true distance;[25] but they then approach with great rapidity. This illusion may contribute to road accidents during fog.

Divers are affected by distortions of similar origin, though the effects are usually different along and across the line of sight. If the object appears to be beyond its physical distance, then (as in a fog) its apparent speed will be increased. If (as is often the case in clear water at close distances) the object appears both nearer than its physical distance and enlarged, there will be different speed distortions depending on the line of travel. An object travelling across the line of sight will appear to move too fast; but one travelling along the line of sight, over an apparently short distance, will appear to move too slowly. An object moving diagonally, or moving from the region where it appears too near to the region where it appears too far, would of course vary from slow to fast. Divers adapt to these speed distortions after some time in the water,[26] presumably as a result of adapting to the distance and size distortions.

Speed distortions are also caused by mirrors which magnify or minify. Aircraft pilots learn to cope with the magnification caused by periscopes,[27] and drivers can cope with the minification caused by some car wing mirrors.

VII   *Correction for Bodily Movement*

Most of the effects mentioned so far can occur when the observer is stationary. Additional illusions can arise when the observer moves, or travels in a moving vehicle. There are two important differences between moving in a vehicle, and moving around on our own feet: vehicle movement is usually fast and passive, while bodily movement is slow and active. We can normally correct quite well for our own bodily movements, so that we see stationary objects as stationary despite our movements; but if we move fast our correction system cannot cope, and we see the world as moving. In vehicles, we move both fast and passively; and both these factors prevent us from correcting adequately. Consequently, we see the world rush past when travelling in a car or train. However we do apply some correction for fast vehicle travel, as can be seen from the greater apparent speed of the outside world when travelling backwards than when travelling forwards: this suggests that some correction is made for the normal forwards direction of travel, and appreciably less for the backwards direction. Similarly, subjects who are moved passively on a swing in the dark show greater size-constancy (for an illuminated circle) when moving forwards rather than backwards.[28] This makes the same point – that people are more able to correct for forwards than backwards movement, even when it is passive movement.

Sometimes one may fail to make adequate correction even for slow, active movement. S. P. Thompson wrote: 'Underneath the famous Suspension Bridge (at Clifton) a zigzag path winds up to the top of the cliff, shaded overhead by trees. Walking up this path you see the bridge at intervals between the boughs, and, as the body rises and falls with the motion of each step, the bridge appears to be swaying violently up and down, as if it were blown about in the wind.'[4]

When movement is both passive and unexpected, correction is poor and the flow-patterns of the retinal stimulus can be very confusing. This situation often occurs for a diver in a rough sea: he is swept over rocks, shifting sand, or waving seaweed, and may have the impression that he is stationary and the whole world moving in an unpredictable manner. During active swimming a diver corrects quite well for his own movement, provided there are no currents. He may, however, make errors during ascents and descents if he is not neutrally buoyant: he corrects for his intended rate of swimming rather than his actual rate.[29] If he is overweight he may sink whilst trying to ascend; and *vice versa* when underweight. If there are few visual cues, he may be slow to realise that he is moving in the wrong direction.

VIII *Flow-patterns*

The flow-pattern of the outside world, as one travels in a vehicle, is quite complex (Fig. 6.1). When looking out of the side windows, the foreground rushes past in the opposite direction, the midground moves more slowly, and the background very slowly. The relative movement of objects at different distances is known as *motion parallax*. The nature of the flow-pattern changes with the fixation distance, everything appearing to flow round the spot at which the observer is looking. If the observer watches the midground, the foreground will rush past him, the midground appear almost stationary, and the background will apparently move in the same direction as the vehicle. A similar effect occurs when looking out of the front of a car; mountains on the distant horizon may appear to retreat, in contrast to the rapidly-approaching foreground. At the same time the horizon may appear to sink, as trees and hills in the foreground continually rise to obscure the view.

The flow-pattern is of great importance to aircraft pilots making a visual landing. If the plane is descending at a constant speed and slope, the touchdown point will appear stationary, while all other objects expand from this point at different velocities. The expansion-pattern varies with the speed, glide slope, and plane attitude. Height alone does not change the expansion pattern, though the apparent velocity of any object on the ground increases as the height is reduced. Pilots can learn to use the apparent movement of objects as a cue to distance.[10]

When driving at night, the moon often appears to glide through the sky at the same speed as the car. It might be thought that

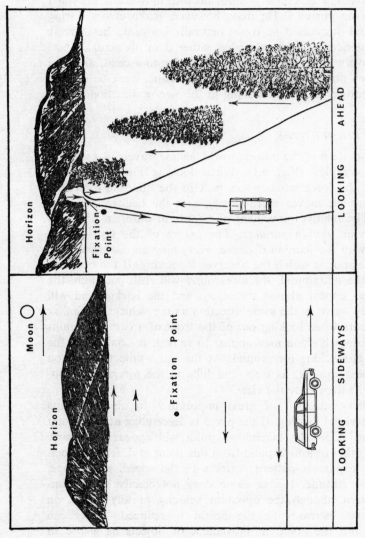

FIGURE 6.1

Flow patterns during travel in a car. The arrow head represents the direction of apparent motion, and the length of the shaft represents the apparent speed. The apparent motion changes direction beyond the fixation point.

this is another example of the flow-pattern, or of induced movement, the moon apparently travelling with the car in contrast
to the landscape rushing backwards. However, the apparent
movement can occur when the moon is quite high in the sky,
and the landscape barely visible. The probable explanation is
that the observer makes a perceptual correction for the apparent
speed of his own car: any object which keeps pace with him
must appear to move at about the same speed. This is a fair
assumption for close objects, such as planes in the sky; but it
is untrue for distant celestial objects.

IX   *Apparent Speed In Cars*

We make use of many different sorts of cues to judge the speed
of a car in which we are travelling. We use visual cues from the
flow-pattern of the surrounding scenery; auditory cues from the
note of the engine, and from echoes; and bodily cues from
vibration and acceleration. Despite all these cues, our ability
to judge speed is not very high. Evans[30] found that practised
drivers could make fairly accurate estimates of their own speed,
when allowed both vision and hearing; but when the sounds
were removed, they always underestimated their speed. Cohen
and his colleagues[31] found systematic tendencies to over- and
under-estimation among drivers, according to speed, acceleration
and deceleration; and likewise, though with rather different
trends, among passengers.

We tend to adapt to the speed at which we are travelling, so
that any change seems exaggerated. This was confirmed by
Denton,[32] even when the initial speed was held for only a few
seconds. When drivers were asked to reduce speed to a half or
a quarter of their present speed, they drove too fast. For
example, a driver approaching a roundabout at 60 m.p.h.
(97 k.p.h.) who wishes to halve his speed, is likely to enter the
roundabout at 38 m.p.h. (61 k.p.h.). The converse is true of a
driver entering a motorway from a slip road: if he approaches
at 25 m.p.h. (40 k.p.h.) and wishes to double his speed, he is
likely to achieve only 38 m.p.h. (61 k.p.h.) on entering.

Speed adaptation is due to the rapid adaptation of the vestibular system; and to the partial adaptation of the visual system

to the flow-pattern. However, if the visual cues are suddenly increased, the driver will tend to slow down. Drivers will reduce their speed by an extra 10 to 15 per cent on approaching a roundabout, if a pattern of narrow transverse yellow lines is painted on the approach road.[33] Auditory stimuli have also been used with success; grooves in the road can provide an 'audible warning strip', fast cars making an unpleasant sound on crossing the grooves.[31]

In a fog, forward visibility is very much reduced; but the flow-pattern at the side may give drivers sufficient cues to enable them to navigate bends at speeds as high as 40 m.p.h. (64 k.p.h.).[34] The driver may well be tempted to drive faster than is safe, in order to integrate the visual cues into an adequate flow-pattern. In the absence of a flow-pattern, the driver may not realise how fast he is going; and if he does notice an impoverished flow-pattern, it may suggest to him that he is travelling much slower than is actually the case. This may be one contributory factor to 'motorway madness', or reckless driving in a fog.

X Acceleration and Movement Illusions

Drivers and passengers are often subjected to sudden changes in the speed or direction of travel. The accelerative forces stimulate the vestibular system, and give rise to illusions of movement, tilt, size and distance. The illusions are probably due to false sensations of body movement, for which the brain mistakenly corrects; but the precise mechanism is unclear.

Some confusion is caused by differences in the targets which subjects watch during acceleration experiments. The targets discussed here are lights glowing in the dark, which are attached to the framework of the vehicle: in this case the target remains at a constant distance from the subject, apart from any eye-movements which he makes. Some authors refer to after-images (the after-effect of staring at a bright light): after-images are confusing, because they sometimes appear to move in the same direction as real objects, and sometimes in the opposite direction, depending upon what the subject watches. Accelerative illusions are not very effective in broad daylight, but are quite likely to occur at night when watching the lights on the instrument panel of a car or plane.

The *oculogravic illusion* has already been described (Ch. 5, Section II). Horizontal linear acceleration alters the effective direction of the gravitational force, causing an upright passenger to feel tilted and to see the visual world as tilted. Apparent movement occurs when the accelerative force changes, and objects appear to swing into a new orientation. The direction of movement depends on the orientation of the passenger, and can be very complicated during aircraft manœuvres.[2, 10] Some changes in apparent distance or size may also occur.[35]

Linear acceleration can also operate in a vertical direction, causing the *elevator illusion*.[2, 10] This is also known as the *oculoagravic illusion*, which is a misleading name as it implies that the illusion is connected with zero gravity. In fact, it may happen during any change in the normal force of gravity, such as is caused by adding or subtracting an accelerative force to the earth's gravitational force. Such changes occur during parabolic flights (which give forces between 0–3 g), and at the stop and start of a lift. The effective force increases when the lift accelerates on the way up or decelerates on the way down; and it decreases when the lift decelerates on the way up or accelerates on the way down. Under increasing g the framework of the lift appears to rise for a moment, while under decreasing g it appears to sink. People who are frequently subjected to large accelerations in lifts, such as miners, claim that the illusion disappears with experience.[36]

The *oculogyral illusion*[2, 10] is caused by angular acceleration. When a person is rotated to the left, a target fixed in front of his eyes appears to swing to the left, and then gradually return to centre. If the rotation continues at a constant rate, the target remains motionless. When the rotation slows down suddenly, the target swings to the right; this direction of apparent rotation may continue as an after-effect for thirty or forty seconds after bodily rotation has ceased, though oscillations of direction sometimes occur. The opposite effects happen with rightward rotation.

The after-effect of rotation can cause trouble to pilots – when they come out of a spin, they sometimes feel as if they are spinning in the opposite direction. They may then try to counteract this, and go back into the original spin – a situation known as 'graveyard spin'. Luckily, repeated exposure to rotation produces some adaptation.[10]

It is often claimed that movement illusions associated with acceleration are due to the reflex eye-movements (vestibular nystagmus) which occur in response to vestibular stimulation. The argument runs thus: the reflex eye-movements are involuntary, so the brain fails to correct for them; hence objects which remain stationary with respect to the observer (such as the vehicle in which he travels) appear to move in the opposite direction to his eye-movements. Eye-movements of approximately the required type undoubtedly occur; but it is not clear that they are the cause of the movement illusions. The correlation between the actual eye-movements and the perceived movement is poor.[37] Moreover, most types of reflex eye-movements cause no illusions, as the brain corrects for them quite adequately: it would, therefore, be necessary to make a special case for vestibular nystagmus – and the reasoning becomes circular. Eye-movement theories are also useless at explaining the associated illusions of tilt, size and distance[35, 38] that occur under certain types of acceleration. Neither can they explain the audiogyral[39] and audiogravic[40] illusions – changes in the apparent source of a sound which occur under acceleration. It is more likely that all these illusions are due to changes in the felt position of the body. The brain miscalculates at first, when subjected to new methods of travel; but the illusions disappear when the brain learns to associate the vestibular stimuli with the appropriate visual and other stimuli.

XI *Motion Sickness*

Motion sickness is a problem – particularly to passengers; drivers are less susceptible, as they are in a better position to anticipate the changes in accelerative forces. The sickness is often so severe as to make the sufferer helpless during the attack, and to leave him weak afterwards. Seasickness is especially dangerous to divers, since vomiting in the mouthpiece of the breathing apparatus is often fatal.

The main cause of motion sickness seems to be a complex

series of changes in the type of acceleration to which the person is subjected. The changes, and the sickness, are exacerbated if the person moves his head while the vehicle is moving.[41] If the head is moved, movement effects known as the *Coriolis illusion* or *vestibular coriolis reaction* may occur.[42] Normally the brain discounts the vestibular sensations of acceleration that result from voluntary head movements, provided the body is stationary or moving slowly. The trouble arises when the passenger is travelling fast, particularly with irregular movement. In this case the passenger feels his body moving when his head moves, and may see glowing lights apparently move.

Adaptation can occur to situations which tend to produce motion sickness. Sailors eventually 'find their sea legs', and subjects who live in rotating rooms for a few days become less susceptible to sickness and coriolis illusions.[43] Naturally, adaptation to unusual vestibular stimulation leads to an after-effect: people who have been at sea for a few days sometimes experience feelings equivalent to seasickness on land, the world apparently swaying as they walk. Repeated alternation between land and sea leads to a reduction of both seasickness and after-effects. Adaptation to motion sickness seems to be fairly specific to one type of motion – any change in the pattern of motion can bring on renewed sickness. Adaptation is not like a travel drug, which works in a general manner to counteract all types of motion sickness.

Vestibular stimulation is not the only cause of motion sickness. Films can make an audience feel very queasy if they show sequences taken from a car or plane during violent movements. Some suggestible people also become sick at the smell of oil, or the sight of a bus; but such people are quite easily cured by charms (such as sitting on brown paper, or dangling chains from the back of the car), provided that they believe the charms to be effective.

In most cases motion sickness seems to be due to a mismatch between the current stimulation from the visual, vestibular, and other sensory systems, and the pattern of stimulation expected on the basis of past experience.[44]

XII *Pressure Vertigo*

A hazard which affects both divers and aircraft pilots is *pressure vertigo* (or *alternobaric vertigo*), a sensation of dizziness or spinning which can occur on failure to 'clear the ears' properly during changes in pressure. It was observed as early as 1896 in caisson workers.[45] Divers experience more rapid pressure changes than pilots, so tend to have a higher incidence of attacks – about 26 per cent of divers are susceptible,[46] and 17 per cent of jet pilots.[47]

Vertigo most frequently occurs on the ascent, or after a violent Valsalva manœuvre (an attempt to clear the ears by breathing out into a pinched nose). Under these circumstances, air of relatively high pressure is trapped for a short while in the middle ear. It seems likely that the pressure differential excites the vestibular system in a way that simulates the effects of rotation; but the exact mechanism is unclear.[48]

Pressure vertigo normally produces a sensation of spinning or tumbling, which fades within a minute. It is usually accompanied by vestibular nystagmus, and by apparent movement of surrounding objects. Pilots often see the aircraft as rotating with them. Divers report mainly bodily sensations of rotation; but if there are any objects visible in front of them, then these also appear to rotate with them.

Most cases of pressure vertigo seem to be due to difficulty in clearing one ear, or to greater difficulty with one ear than the other. There are few published accounts which attempt to link the direction of apparent rotation with the side of the most troublesome ear. However, many anecdotal reports from divers suggest that a blocked left ear causes apparent anti-clockwise rotation, and a blocked right ear clockwise rotation. This seems to be true whether the diver is ascending or descending. In addition, there are some reports of tumbling, tilting, and other sensations; so the general rule cannot be quite as simple as just stated.

Unlike motion sickness – and several other types of movement illusion – pressure vertigo is not reduced by experience. Its onset is sudden and unpredictable, and no learning is possible.

The only sense in which adaptation could be said to occur is that the sufferer becomes less anxious on subsequent occasions, and shows less behavioural disruption. This latter topic – adaptation to dangerous situations – is considered in more detail in the last chapter.

NOTES

1   D. E. Johannsen, 'Early history of perceptual illusions', *J. History of the Behavioural Sciences*, 1971, Vol. 7, pp. 127–40.
2   For a review containing both early and modern references see J. O. Robinson, *The Psychology of Visual Illusion*, London: Hutchinson, 1972.
3   R. Addams, 'An account of a peculiar optical phaenomenon seen after looking at a moving body, etc.', *Philosophical Magazine*, 1834, Vol. 5, pp. 373–4.
4   S. P. Thompson, 'Some new optical illusions', *Journal of Science*, 1879, Vol. 9, pp. 234–40.
5   S. P. Thompson, 'Optical illusions of motion', *Brain*, 1880, Vol. 3, pp. 289–98.
6   H. B. Barlow and R. M. Hill, 'Evidence for a physiological explanation of the waterfall phenomenon and figural after-effects', *Nature*, 1963, Vol. 200, pp. 1345–7.
7   R. W. Wood, 'The "haunted-swing" illusion', *Psychol. Rev.*, 1895, Vol. 2, pp. 277–8.
8   W. H. Murray, *Mountaineering in Scotland*, London: Dent, 1947, pp. 140 and 214.
9   L. Brosgole, R. M. Cristal and O. Carpenter, 'The role of eye movements in the perception of visually induced motion', *Percept. Psychophys.*, 1968, Vol. 3, pp. 166–8.
10 D. G. Pitts, 'Visual illusions and aircraft accidents', SAM–TR–67–28, U.S.A.F. School of Aerospace Medicine, Brooks Air Force Base, Texas, 1967. This paper also contains a detailed analysis of flow-patterns when flying.
11 T. Holzel, 'The Mystery of Mallory and Irvine', *Mountain*, 1971, Vol. 17, pp. 30–5.
12 H. Ruttledge, *Everest 1933*, London: Hodder & Stoughton, 1934, p. 152.
13 R. L. Gregory and O. L. Zangwill, 'The origin of the autokinetic effect', *Q.J. exp. Psychol.*, 1963, Vol. 15, pp. 252–61.
14 C. Shopland and R. L. Gregory, 'The effect of touch on a visually ambiguous three-dimensional figure', *Q.J. exp. Psychol.*, 1964, Vol. 16, pp. 66–70.
15 A. Ames Jr., 'Visual perception and the rotating trapezoidal window', *Psychol. Monogr.*, 1951, Vol. 65, Whole No. 324.
16 G. W. Allport and T. F. Pettigrew, 'Cultural influence on the per-

ception of movement: the trapezoidal illusion among Zulus', *J. abnorm. soc. Psychol.*, 1957, Vol. 55, pp. 104–13.

17 R. H. Day and R. P. Power, 'Apparent reversal (oscillation) of rotary motion in depth: An investigation and a general theory', *Psychol. Rev.*, 1965, Vol. 72, pp. 117–27.

18 P. A. Kolers, 'Some differences between real and apparent visual movement', *Vision Research*, 1963, Vol. 3, pp. 91–206.

19 J. P. Frisby, 'Real and apparent movement – same or different mechanisms', *Vision Research*, 1971, Vol. 12, pp. 1051–5.

20 I. Rock and S. Ebenholtz, 'Stroboscopic movement based on change of phenomenal rather than retinal location', *Amer. J. Psychol.*, Vol. 75, pp. 193–207.

21 M. Minnaert, *Light and Colour in the Open Air* (trans. H. M. Kremer-Priest; revised K. E. Brian Jay), London: Bell, 1959.

22 I. Rock, A. Lewis Hill and M. Fineman, 'Speed constancy as a function of size constancy', *Percept. Psychophys.*, 1968, Vol. 4, pp. 37–40.

23 J. F. Brown, 'The visual perception of velocity', *Psychol. Forsch.*, 1931, Vol. 14, pp. 199–232.

24 J. H. Fremlin, 'Motion stereoscopy', *Nature*, 1972, Vol. 238, pp. 406–7.

25 H. E. Ross, 'Water, fog and the size-distance invariance hypothesis', *Brit. J. Psychol.*, 1967, Vol. 58, pp. 301–13.

26 H. E. Ross and M. H. Rejman, 'Adaptation to speed distortions under water', *Brit. J. Psychol.*, 1972, Vol. 63, pp. 257–64.

27 S. N. Roscoe, S. G. Hasler and D. J. Dougherty, 'Flight by periscope: making take-offs and landings: the influence of image magnification, practice, and various conditions of flight', *Human Factors*, Vol. 8, pp. 13–40.

28 R. L. Gregory and H. E. Ross, 'Visual constancy during movement: 1. Effects of S's forward and backward movement on size constancy', *Percept. Mot. Skills*, 1964, Vol. 18, pp. 3–8.

29 H. E. Ross and P. Lennie, 'Visual stability during bodily movement underwater', *Underwater Ass. Rep.*, 1968, Vol. 3, pp. 55–7.

30 L. Evans, 'Speed estimation from a moving automobile', *Ergonomics*, 1970, Vol. 13, pp. 219–30.

31 J. Cohen and B. Preston, *Causes and Prevention of Road Accidents*, London: Faber & Faber, 1968.

32 G. G. Denton, 'The effect of speed and speed change on drivers' speed judgement', RRL Rep. LR97, 1967, Road Research Laboratory, Crowthorne, Berks.

33 *The Guardian,* 15 January 1972.

34 R. L. Moore and H. P. Ruffell-Smith, 'Ergonomics and safety in motor car design', *I. Mech. Eng.*, Paper No. 6, London, 1966.

35 A. G. Goldstein, 'Linear acceleration and apparent distance', *Percept. Mot. Skills*, 1959, Vol. 9, pp. 267–9.

36 A miner speaking on B.B.C. Radio 4 at 20.10 hours, 11 August 1972.

37 G. H. Byford, 'Eye movements and the optogyral illusion', *Aerospace Med.*, 1963, Vol. 34, pp. 119–23; A. A. J. Van Egmond, J. J. Goren and L. B. W. Jongkees, 'Positional nystagmus of

peripheral origin', *J. Physiol.*, (London), 1950, Vol. 110, pp. 447–9; T. C. D. Whiteside, A. Graybiel and J. I. Niven, 'Visual illusions of movement', *Brain*, 1965, Vol. 88, pp. 193–210.

38 R. L. Gregory, J. G. Wallace and F. W. Campbell, 'Changes in the size and shape of visual after-images observed in complete darkness during changes of position in space', *Q.J. exp. Psychol.*, 1959, Vol. 11, pp. 54–5; T. C. D. Whiteside and F. W. Campbell, 'Size constancy effect during angular and radial acceleration', *Q.J. exp. Psychol.*, 1959, Vol. 11, p. 249.

39 B. Clark and A. Graybiel, 'The effect of angular acceleration on sound localisation: the audiogyral illusion', *J. Psychol.*, 1949, Vol. 28, pp. 235–44.

40 A. Graybiel and J. I. Niven, 'The effect of a change in direction of resultant force on sound localization: the audiogravic illusion', *J. exp. Psychol.*, 1951, Vol. 42, pp. 227–30.

41 W. H. Johnson and N. B. G. Taylor, 'Some experiments on the relative effectiveness of various types of accelerations on motion sickness', *Aerospace Med.*, 1961, Vol. 32, pp. 205–8.

42 F. E. Guedry and E. K. Montague, 'Quantitative evaluation of the vestibular coriolis reaction', *Aerospace Med.*, 1961, Vol. 32, pp. 487–500.

43 A. Graybiel, B. Clark and J. J. Zarriello, 'Observations on human subjects, living in a slow rotation room for periods of two days' *Arch. Neurol. London*, 1960, Vol. 3, pp. 55–73.

44 J. T. Reason, 'Motion sickness – some theoretical considerations', *Int. J. Man–Machine Studies*, 1969, Vol. 1, pp. 21–38.

45 F. Alt, 'Über apoplectiforme Labyrintherkrankungen bei Caissonarbeitern', *Monatsschrift Ohrenheilkunde*, 1896, Vol. 30, pp. 341–9; W. Friedrich and F. Tausk, 'Die Erkrankung der Caissonarbeiter (Caissonkrankheit)', *Wien Klin. Rundschau*, 1896, Vol. 10, pp. 233–324.

46 C. E. G. Lundgren, 'Alternobaric vertigo – A diving hazard', *Brit. Med. J.*, 1965, Vol. 2, pp. 511–13.

47 C. E. G. Lundgren and L. U. Malm, 'Alternobaric vertigo among pilots', *Aerospace Med.*, 1966, Vol. 37, pp. 178–80.

48 L. J. Enders and E. Rodriguez-Lopez, 'Aeromedical consultation service case report. Alternobaric vertigo', *Aerospace Med.*, 1970, Vol. 41, pp. 200–2.

CHAPTER 7

The Perception of Danger

Strange environments have an air of the unknown – an aroma that entices some and repels others. Danger itself is an elusive quality, lying partly in the environment and partly in the participant. The subjective element in the perception of danger is much larger than in the perception of most other aspects of the environment. Repeated exposure to danger does not necessarily lead to a true appreciation of the hazards, though it does enable people to control their emotional responses in an adaptive manner.

I Defining Danger

A dangerous activity is one in which an unpleasant event has a fairly high probability of occurring. The more dreadful the event, or the higher the probability, the greater the danger.

Much of the disagreement about the degree of danger is due to uncertainty about the probabilities. Insurance companies may have accurate information about the chances of death from road accidents, fires, or rock-climbing; but ordinary individuals do not. Moreover, the chances of an accident for a particular group or for a given individual may be quite different from the average chances for the whole population: young unmarried males, for example, are particularly dangerous drivers. There are some events over which we have almost no control: these include war, earthquakes, storms, droughts, and other 'Acts of God'. Predictable disasters are less dangerous because they can normally be avoided. Skilled mountaineers, for example, can often tell when the snow is likely to avalanche, and keep away from dangerous places. Part of the skill of coping with dangerous environments lies in this ability to predict and avoid.

The skilled person also learns to prevent accidents. He not only avoids trouble, but makes sure that he does not cause it. Given knowledge, physical skill, and good equipment, he can go in safety where others come to grief. The risk that he faces is thus much lower than that of a novice attempting the same thing.

The objective hazard may vary from person to person, but even greater variation is found in the subjective estimates of hazard. The individual has little information about the accident rate for someone of his level of ability in his present situation. A climber, for example, has to weigh up his chances of death by avalanche from his knowledge of present snow conditions and recent climbing deaths. His estimate will probably suffer from 'small sample bias', and be strongly influenced by the most recent events. Accidents tend to occur in bunches; and, if he knows that several competent climbers were recently killed in an avalanche, he may over-estimate his own chances of such a death.

Even if agreement were reached on the probability of an accident, people might still disagree about the danger. Some might feel that the accident is trivial, others that it is dreadful. Some regard death as the ultimate disaster, while others regard it as the gateway to a better life. Some feel that maiming is worse than death, others that life of any sort is precious. Further disagreement can arise when people try to compare a highly probable but small disaster with an improbable but serious one. Given all these types of uncertainty and subjectivity, it is not surprising that danger is hard to measure.

Non-participants often think of those who take part in dangerous activities as being 'risky' or 'hard men'. The 'hard men' may not see themselves that way, because they rate their own chance of an accident as low, or because they are indifferent to the consequences of an accident. In some cases their behaviour is quite rational, because the risk for them really is low, or because they know they are doomed to die of cancer shortly. In other cases, the behaviour seems irrational, or totally 'mad'.

The individual apparently feels himself immune from disaster, or shows no regard for his own life; he suffers from delusions of grandeur, or is gambling with death in an attempted suicide. He may also place a much higher value on success than most people would do. Sometimes the derangement is only temporary: divers suffering from nitrogen narcosis, and drivers under the influence of alcohol, may incur absurd hazards.

Novices do not invariably over-estimate the hazards of a dangerous activity. If it is unspectacular and lacks obvious skill, the hazard may be under-estimated. Mountaineering in Scotland is a case in point: a disproportionately large number of accidents happen to English visitors,[1] who arrive ill-equipped and un-suspecting of the problems that lie ahead. They may be quite competent in their own environment, but have little knowledge of the severity of the weather and the terrain in the higher mountains.

II   *The Assessment of Rock-climbs*

Climbing routes may be difficult or dangerous – or both. Routes are usually graded according to the most difficult pitch (the 'crux') with some allowance for average difficulty, and for the degree of 'exposure'. Exposure is psychological rather than physical: it has to do with such things as lack of protection, and the length of fall should one slip. It is not directly con-cerned with the difficulty of a move; but fear of the outcome may itself increase the difficulty of the move. The objective difficulty of a climb will naturally vary with the weather and the state of the rock-surface, and the subjective difficulty will vary with the competence of the climbers and with their states of mind.

Climbers grade climbs: but the factors mentioned above make it difficult to assign precise grades which are universally accep-table. Several different grading schemes exist, depending on whether the route is a summer rock climb, or a snow and ice climb. The Scottish summer grading scheme runs: Easy, Moderate, Difficult, Very Difficult, Severe and Very Severe. Some climbers attempt to subdivide these grades even further. This is probably futile, since people cannot make systematic use of more than about seven categories.[2] However, climbing standards have risen since the categories were first adopted, so that 'Difficult' is now considered 'easy', even though the original name is retained for the grade. Serious climbers are only interested in 'Very Difficult' and above, so there is some excuse for subdivision of the higher grades.

There may be several reasons for questioning the existing grades of certain climbs. The route itself may become easier or more difficult due to wear and tear; and the climber who first graded the route may have had excessively high or low standards.

Climbing a new route is always more difficult than following a known one, so there is a temptation to overgrade new climbs.

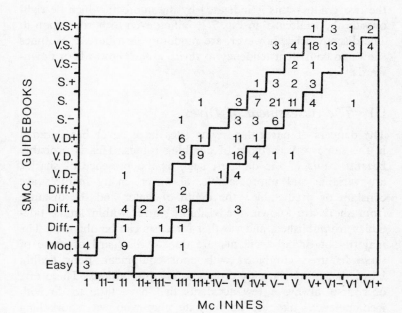

FIGURE 7.1

Scatter diagram showing the number of climbs receiving a given combination of grades in the S.M.C. guides (Scottish system) and McInnes (Alpine system). Points lying outside the 'staircase' show poor agreement between the two grades. (After P. Murray-Rust and J. D. Evans, unpublished diagram.)

Overgrading is very irritating for subsequent climbers, who had hoped for something more exciting.[3] Undergrading is a more dangerous practice, as it can lead inexperienced climbers into difficult situations.

Naturally, the original gradings do not go unchallenged, and revised guide books sometimes alter them, or at least change the rank order of routes within a grade. A wide range of climbs and guide books is shown in Fig. 7.1. This compares the gradings given by McInnes[4] in 1971 with those found in the most recent editions of the Scottish Mountaineering Club District Guides. McInnes uses the grading system of the International Union of Alpine Clubs: this gives grades I–VI, which correspond approximately to the British grades Easy Hard Very Severe.[5] About 7 per cent of the climbs show a large discrepancy between the two grades – this is indicated by the numbers which lie right outside the 'staircase' in Fig. 7.1, failing even to border upon it. The discrepancies, however, are randomly distributed: McInnes shows no consistent tendency to revise grades upwards or downwards.

III *The Assessment of Dives*

The dangers of particular diving sites have never been graded in the same way as those of climbing routes. This is probably because some of the dangers, such as the presence of sharks, are variable and unpredictable. However, many features are constant or predictable: the depth of water and the distance from shore are known, the visibility varies within limits, tide-tables are published, and weather forecasts can be obtained. The majority of diving accidents are due to disregard of some of these features, combined with poor equipment, poor health, inexperience and lack of proper safety precautions. There are, of course, always a few accidents that have little to do with incompetence – like the unfortunate man who was snorkelling in the Mediterranean, inhaled a bee down his snorkel, was stung on the back of the throat, and died of suffocation from the swelling.[6]

Some hazards are physiological, and are not directly related to a particular diving site. For example, decompression sickness

(Ch. 2) is likely to occur if the diver stays too deep for too long, or ascends too fast. The chances of an attack of 'the bends' vary greatly from person to person, and from time to time. Nevertheless, tables have been drawn up which list 'safe' procedures for decompression on the ascent, or which give the maximum depth and length of dive which can be undertaken without the necessity to decompress. The rules – or the grading of the dangers involved – vary in different diving organisations. Some divers are prepared to take greater risks than others. Commercial divers are usually riskier than sports divers: they want to stay down as long as possible, for financial reasons. They

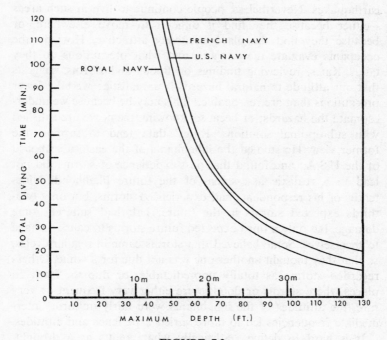

FIGURE 7.2

'No-stop curves' according to the rules of three Navies. The curves give the maximum permissible total diving time, without decompression stops, for various maximum depths reached. The allowable 'bottom time' can be calculated by subtracting a descent time (at 100 ft per minute) and an ascent time (at 60 ft per minute). (After L. Kenyon, *Aqualung Diving*, London: Allen & Unwin, 1970.)

prefer to use the French Navy decompression tables, which are more 'generous' than those of the U.S. Navy or the Royal Navy. Sports divers generally use the more conservative British tables. The 'No-stop Curves' for the French, American and British Navies are shown in Fig. 7.2. The higher French curve gives permission to stay down longer at a given depth without stopping to decompress.

IV Attitudes to Environmental Hazards

Some parts of the world are more hazardous than others, in that there is a greater likelihood of floods, droughts, hurricanes and earthquakes. Nevertheless, people continue to live in such areas – either because they find it difficult to move elsewhere, or because they find the place positively attractive. How do the occupants evaluate the dangers, and what precautions do they take? Kates, reviewing findings on floods and storms, suggests that our attitude to natural hazards is unrealistic: we take fewer precautions than are reasonable.[7] This may be because we underestimate the hazards; or because, knowing them, we are satisfied with sub-optimal solutions. Kates' data tend to support the former view. He studied the inhabitants of the eastern seaboard of the U.S.A., and found that past experience of storms did not lead to a realistic assessment of the future likelihood. Nine-tenths of his respondents had experienced storms, but only two-thirds expected storms in the future; half had suffered some damage, but only a third expected future storms to cause damage to themselves. Some believed that storms came in regular cycles, so that they thought another one was not due for a while. Others regarded storms as totally unpredictable, or due to 'fate'. In places where storms or floods were either very frequent or very rare, the attitudes of the inhabitants were fairly uniform; intermediate frequencies led to more varied experience and attitudes.

It is hard to define statistically what counts as a drought. Saarinen[8] studied the attitudes of farmers living in the Great Plains of the U.S.A., in areas of varying degrees of aridity. Farmers in all areas tended to under-estimate the frequency of droughts; but those in the more arid regions considered a smaller reduction in rain to be a drought, and predicted more droughts.

They were also more inclined to believe in the possibility of increasing the supply of water by techniques such as 'water witching' or 'weather modification'.[9]

Most people like their home environment, however unattractive or dangerous it may appear to outsiders. They become attached not only to their companions, but to the scenery and to the way of life that the scenery dictates. Sonnenfeld,[10] for example, confirmed that the natives of Alaska preferred their own type of landscape – though the women liked slightly warmer and more vegetated environments than the men. Short-stay workers showed more varied attitudes: male teachers were the most satisfied with the rugged and cold environment, and technicians the least. Sonnenfeld suggests that it may be necessary to pay high salaries to visiting technicians, since they lack the motives that attract teachers, scientists and missionaries.

Within Britain there is considerable agreement about the most desirable areas to live in. The South is generally considered highly desirable, except for London; the Lake District is also desirable, but otherwise the further North the less desirable. This was demonstrated by Gould and White[11] on the basis of the average rankings of areas by school-leavers all over Britain, corrected for local bias. However, this average order is normally modified by a strong preference for one's own local area, and by sharp discrimination between other areas near home. The local preferences of southerners coincide fairly well with average national preferences; but further north the 'national map' is severely distorted by local preferences. Thus children from Kirkwall (Orkney Islands) think that the Orkneys are the best place to live, and that Caithness and Aberdeen are highly desirable; they also find Scotland generally preferable to England or Wales. Nevertheless, their assessment of the *relative desirability* of areas within England and Wales is much the same as the British average.

Environmental hazards may be perceived as slight not only because the probabilities of disasters are under-estimated, but because people become habituated to certain kinds of disaster. Familiar types of death seem less serious than unfamiliar ones. Deaths from old age, lung cancer and heart attacks seem 'normal'; while death from an unknown or very rare illness

seems more dreadful. Car accidents and drownings are unpleasant to think about, but their regular occurrence reduces the
'impact'. The deaths seem worse if many people are killed in one
accident, or if the victims are young, or if the accident coincides
with a national holiday, or if it occurs near home.

V *The Assignment of Blame for an Accident*

The desire to find a scapegoat for a 'serious' accident is almost
universal. One tends to feel easier if one can pinpoint a cause
and blame an individual. Possibly this action makes one feel
safer: if one knows the cause one can avoid such dangers oneself and protect others from them. One may also want to
condemn or punish the culprit, in order to dissuade him from
dangerous behaviour in the future, or to exact retribution on
behalf of the victim.

Unfortunately, accidents usually have several origins, and no
one person is particularly blameworthy. The way in which we
assign blame is often biassed and unfair.[12] For example, high-
status people are considered more responsible for their own
actions than low-status people, provided the actions are good.
If the actions are dubious, they are considered more 'justifiable'
when they originate from high-status individuals. Blame depends
not only on the status of the actors, but on the seriousness of
the outcome: minor events are attributed to 'chance', disastrous
events to some causal agent. Actions that would normally be
considered 'reasonable' may become 'blameworthy' after a bad
accident. For example, if a parked car runs away the driver is
considered more culpable if a person is injured than if the car
alone is damaged.[13] People are also illogical in the way they
assess evidence: when considering a motor accident, for example,
they are more impressed by the *total* number of witnesses holding one or other opinion than they are by the *relative* numbers
on each side.[14]

A mountaineering accident illustrates some points in the
assignment of blame. The climber Walter Bonatti became
separated from two inexperienced companions in bad weather
on Mont Blanc; they took a dangerous route and died. Bonatti
complained that he was blamed for losing them, when he had

behaved in a manner that would normally be considered prudent and proper if no deaths had occurred. The accident, he maintained, was the fault of the victims: instead of following him to safety, they deliberately chose a different route.[15] This illustrates the point that the *victim* of an accident is sometimes regarded as blameworthy, or at least partially 'deserving' of his fate.[16]

It is not socially acceptable to speak ill of the dead, particularly of the famous. Those who court danger once too often are usually said to be the victims of cruel fate. For example, Ian Breach wrote of the racing driver Bruce McLaren: 'A current theme ran through the many tributes that were made to him last night: he was superbly safe on the track, and knew his machine down to the last nut and bolt. A freak mechanical failure was held to be the only conceivable cause of the accident.'[17]

The survivors of accidents are in a very difficult position, and tend to blame fate, or anyone rather than themselves. Mountaineers sometimes regard the mountain as having a mystical power of its own. Thus when Brian Nally was rescued from the Eiger in 1962 after his companion, Barry Brewster, had been swept to his death, he said: 'It's a pig of a face, but somehow it's the final test of how good you are . . . now I know that it is better than us.'[18] Similarly, climbers in less serious difficulties use the phrase 'It won't go' when a rock face is beyond their abilities.

Other survivors have occasionally been known to choose a novel way of clearing themselves of blame: they refuse to admit that the accident occurred. Whether or not they really believe their own story, they try to convince others of its truth. For example, a man was found suffering from exposure in Glen Lyon, and he insisted that he was actually in Glen Lochay, his destination; he even wrote a letter to the local paper stating that he was not lost, and had been found almost within sight of his father's car in Glen Lochay.[19] Divers who get 'the bends' are also likely to prevaricate: they sometimes deny having broken the decompression rules, and maintain that their case is exceptional, or even that they are suffering from some entirely different form of paralysis. It is rare, but refreshing, to hear of individuals who accept full responsibility for accidents: 'If responsibility means anything, I was responsible for those boys, and I am not bringing them back' said the master in charge during a glissading tragedy on Snowdon.[20]

VI   *Danger as a Motive*

Some people enjoy dangerous activities because of the risks. They enjoy the exhilarating feeling of arousal and the sense of superiority that comes from seeming riskier than other people. Those who approve of risky behaviour may call it 'courage' and those who disapprove 'foolhardiness'. Attitudes vary with the context: we disapprove of dangerous driving, approve of acts of heroism, and are in two minds about mountaineering.

The feeling that risk is a virtue may be one reason why people are so reluctant to use safety devices such as seat-belts,[21] crash-helmets and life-jackets. Complete safety precautions are often cumbersome and inconvenient; they may also reduce a spontaneous adventure to the level of a pre-programmed moon-walk.[22]

Laboratory experiments on risk-taking tell us little about the danger motive in real life. There are many different kinds of risks, and people do not respond in the same way to all of them.[23] Laboratory experiments are usually concerned with gambling and decision-making, where the probabilities and the financial rewards can be specified exactly. In real life, neither the probabilities, nor the value of the rewards and penalties, can be measured precisely. The rewards and penalties are also different in kind: the subject in a psychological experiment stands to gain nothing but a little money and to lose nothing but the possibility of more money; in real life he may stand to win or lose a fortune, and he may risk death for the sake of glory. Risk-taking may be quite different when the rewards and costs are high than when they are low.

Laboratory experiments frequently demonstrate the 'risky-shift' phenomenon: group risk-taking tends to be more risky than the average behaviour of individuals alone.[23] The reason for this is not clear: risk-taking may seem more virtuous in public; risky people may be more persuasive than timid people; or the group situation may alter the subjective values of the probabilities, rewards and penalties. Whatever the explanation, it has not been established that the 'risky-shift' occurs in physically dangerous situations in real life. Do groups of climbers go on when the majority would have preferred to turn back? Or do they reluctantly retreat for the sake of the timid minority? Brown[24] suggests that the 'risky-shift' may apply to car driving, drivers in a group being inclined to imitate the overtaking habits of the more powerful cars. There are, of course, other contributory factors during crowded traffic conditions; frustration of previous attempts to overtake, habituation to risk after prolonged driving, and the danger of being rammed from behind in a fog, may all lead to risky overtaking.

When the penalties are small, risky behaviour can be very useful in discovering the limits of one's abilities. This is true of the few real-life experiments which have been conducted – mainly by Cohen and his colleagues.[14] They have investigated such matters as the ability of footballers to estimate their chances of shooting goals from various distances; and the ability of bus drivers to estimate their success at driving through gaps of various sizes (whisky makes them over-optimistic!). Errors in such experiments have fairly trivial consequences. In dangerous activities, where accidents can prove fatal, errors cannot be used as a means of learning the skill: participants have to learn the level of their ability through success rather than through failure.[25] They can, of course, also learn vicariously: the successes and failures of others teach them what is possible. The knowledge that others have climbed a certain rock-face, or been to the moon, makes it much easier for those who follow in subsequent attempts.

VII *'Safe' Motives for Dangerous Activities*

Why do people go diving, parachute-jumping or rock-climbing? 'Because it's there' – Eric Shipton's answer for climbing Everest – is not good enough: people who ask the question want a more rational answer. Yet, perhaps the answer is suitable: it is a silly answer to a silly question. We never question people's motives for activities which are commonplace, or obviously enjoyable; so the act of questioning implies that we think the activity is pointless, unpleasant or foolhardy – 'How could anyone really enjoy hanging on to a freezing rock-face, or diving in cold murky water?' The 'hard man' probably has as many motives for his dangerous sport as the 'ordinary man' has for his choice of work or spouse; and he dislikes having these motives challenged.

If pressed, he may annoy the questioner by saying that he enjoys the activity *because* it is dangerous, or that he enjoys it for its own sake *despite* the danger. Sometimes he will attempt to placate the questioner by admitting that the activity is dangerous and unpleasant, but claiming that it is a means to a worthwhile end – such as scientific knowledge, physical fitness, improvement of the personality, social contact, a sense of achievement, personal or national fame, or financial reward.

The 'character-building' motive is often given as a reason for encouraging children to take up dangerous sports: it is claimed that the activities develop self-confidence, which carries over into normal life. The claim may not be entirely absurd: there is some evidence that training given at Outward Bound Schools may be more effective than conventional methods of curing delinquency.[26] On the other hand, children who voluntarily participate in such activities are usually considered to be 'good' *before* the training. Thus the Very Reverend R. Leonard Small had this to say at the memorial service for five school children and one young leader who died of exposure in the Cairngorms in November 1971: 'These young people deliberately chose, in the middle of winter, to go climbing, rightly or wrongly. They knew it was going to be cold and demand an effort, and they still chose it. I thank God for that spirit. It renews one's faith in the spirit of youth.'[27]

The other type of answer is less popular. It challenges the questioner's prejudices, and implies that the questioner is odd not to have realised that the activity is fun. Instead of rationalising, the 'hard man' invokes some natural instinct. Thus Patey maintains that we enjoy climbing because we inherit the ability from our ape-like ancestors: 'Reverting to nature is generally satisfying . . . physically and psychologically. It may not be ethical . . . but it is usually agreeable . . . In the mountains you can afford to be completely uninhibited. Here, man can act in the manner born, using whatever physical talents nature has bestowed on him. He needs no instruction manuals, no rules and no regulations.'[28] Anderson attempts to explain a much wider range of risky activities by postulating a generalised exploratory urge which he calls the 'Ulysses Factor'.[29] He admits that individual exploits are often useless, but suggests that the urge has adaptive value for the human race: in particular it opens up new territory for an overcrowded species.

Concepts such as 'instinct', 'drive' and 'urge' are not popular in current psychological theories. They are not scientifically testable, and do not help to explain anything. On the other hand, most psychologists would agree that some activities are 'intrinsically motivating' – enjoyable without the expectation of other rewards. Many physical sports and exploratory activities may fall in this category. So may the enjoyment of the beauty of nature – a motive which is frequently invoked by explorers of all types.[22] The emotional appreciation of nature can be observed in young children,[30] and increases with age. In later years it becomes confounded with social factors: adults learn to 'exploit' beautiful scenery for photography, painting or creative writing; or they may pretend to love nature in order to play the role of the 'conservationist' or 'ecologist'.[31]

If the participant feels that an activity is intrinsically enjoyable, or leads to valuable rewards, he will pay to take part; otherwise he will ask to be paid, or wait to be compelled. As one skier said to me when riding a ski-tow in a Cairngorm blizzard, 'If they were paying me to do this instead of me paying them, they'd have to pay me a hell of a lot!' Curiously, people will pay large sums of money to take part in dangerous sports and risky expeditions – activities which would entail special 'hardship' or 'danger' money if paid for professionally. The hardship and danger appear to be attractive in their own right to certain people: they admit the danger, but maintain that they enjoy it.

VIII *Personality, Sex and Dangerous Sports*

What sort of person voluntarily takes part in dangerous sports? Many studies have been made of the personality of sportsmen,[32] but few general conclusions have emerged. The studies suggest that team sportsmen are usually stable extroverts; but that swimmers and athletes are less extroverted, and successful individuals may be positively introverted. A few studies of more dangerous sports have been carried out. For example, Nichols[33] found divers to be more intelligent, affected by feelings, surgent, tough-minded, hard to fool and forthright than the general population; but not as self-sufficient or 'bloody-minded' as climbers. There is also some evidence that successful divers and parachute-jumpers are more extroverted and stable than the general population: such people are less likely to break down under stress than unstable introverts.[34] A criticism that can be made of some of these studies is that they lack suitable control groups: the experimental group may indeed differ in personality from the general population, but this may be due to other factors besides their love of a dangerous sport. For example, Ross[35] found no significant personality differences between student divers and a control sample of students taking the same academic subjects: however, a disproportionately large number of divers took science subjects, and these students were more likely to continue diving than non-scientists. This suggests that an interest in science may be one of the reasons for diving.

The factor that is most strongly correlated with almost all types of sport is sex. Women participate less than men, particularly in dangerous sports such as diving.[35] This may be partly because they are tied to the house with domestic chores and do not have as much spare time as men. It may also be because they tolerate a lower level of risk-taking in physical matters: they are less risky at motor skills,[23] and less risky at car driving.[24] However, the main reason is probably cultural attitudes concerning the sex-role: the 'hard man' role is an acceptable virile role, but there is no equivalent 'hard woman' role. A woman is not supposed to admit to a love of danger or a desire for physical achievement – though she may be allowed occasional acts of heroism towards children. Women, like men, have many motives for taking part in dangerous activities. One of these is social contact, and another social approval. Men gain unequivocal approval for success at a dangerous sport, but successful women

THE PERCEPTION OF DANGER 161

may be accused of masculinity. Naturally, the idea occurs to many women that they might gain more approval if they were *bad* at the sport, or if they made it clear how frightened they were before allowing themselves to succeed. That way they might achieve both social contact and social approval. Women are particularly likely to show such behaviour during mixed-sex climbing or diving expeditions. In practice, this gambit is unlikely to endear them to the other members of the party unless the purpose of the expedition is primarily social in the first place.

IX   *Hallucinations and Stress*

People who spend time alone in dangerous circumstances are liable to have hallucinations. Sometimes these stem from normal perceptual illusions, as described in earlier chapters. In other cases they seem to come entirely from the brain, as there is no external sensory stimulation. For example, experiments on 'sensory deprivation' (in which the subject is isolated from all stimulation for hours on end) have revealed that some people experience hallucinations.[36] Solitary sailors and explorers do not suffer complete sensory deprivation, but they do suffer from social isolation and monotonous surroundings. Single-handed sailors on long voyages are particularly susceptible, as lack of sleep increases the likelihood of hallucinations. Joshua Slocum, for example, used to have visions of a pilot who took over at the helm for him during gales[37] – a reassuring experience. The unfortunate Donald Crowhurst, on the other hand, used to hear sighs when waiting for messages over the radio – these must have seemed like harbingers of doom to his disturbed mind. He was pretending to win a single-handed race round the world when he was in fact stationary: rather than face discovery he jumped overboard.[38]

Auditory errors or hallucinations are such a common experience among isolated people that they may have difficulty in distinguishing between imagination and reality. A tale of this sort was told by members of the Oxford University Expedition to Iceland in 1947: Treloar fell sick, and Swithinbank and Whitehead took him back to base camp, leaving Phizackerley alone on the ice-cap – 'Three days later Whitehead, Swithinbank and Morris returned to the ice-cap. Heavy fog added to the difficulty of finding the camp where Phizackerley was waiting. Having reached the appropriate vicinity of the camp the three set up a horrid yell to which there was no reply. A few minutes later a second yell drew an answer from a very short distance away, and Phizackerley and the camp were quickly found. Having spent most of the previous night shouting in reply to "calls" which proved to be only sounds made by the wind or moving ice, Phizackerley had decided that the first shout was a trick of the imagination.'[39]

Social isolation can lead to symptoms similar to those shown in some kinds of mental illness.[40] Some people develop an 'oceanic' feeling of being 'at one' with the universe; others – particularly aircraft pilots, divers, and people lost in a blizzard – may develop a feeling of 'break-off' or unreality. Prisoners, explorers, and others who have suffered prolonged isolation are often reluctant to talk to ordinary people: they feel unable to carry on a natural conversation, and are frightened of being thought insane.

Many hallucinations are brought on by the tales of others. People expect to see ghosts in 'haunted' houses, a monster in Loch Ness, a Grey Man on Ben MacDhui, and flying saucers in the sky. These 'sightings' often arise from the misinterpretation of natural phenomena, particularly under frightening and ambiguous circumstances. Some people retain a strong belief in these rather improbable phenomena. It has been suggested that belief in Unidentified Flying Objects – and many other 'cranky' attitudes – are the result of social stress: people whose social status is unclear try to escape the norms of society by holding unconventional opinions.[41]

X Emotional Adaptation to Danger

Mild anxiety in a strange situation is probably beneficial. It improves performance at tasks related to safety (Ch. 2); and it encourages caution by biassing perceptual judgements, making things seem more dangerous than they really are. Thus slopes seem steeper, heights higher, depths deeper, precipices nearer and monsters larger than reality. However, extreme anxiety is disruptive, and excessive caution maladaptive; with experience, fearful emotions diminish, and perceptual judgements show more accordance with reality (Chs 3 and 5).

Some of the improvement is due to the learning of new skills: people become more confident as they learn how to cope with new equipment. They may also revise their ideas about the chances of disaster, or discover through experience that a slope is much shallower than they had thought. They may even become indifferent to the thought of certain types of death, and produce rationalisations such as 'Climbing may be dangerous, but it's less dangerous than crossing the road' (an example of the 'lesser peril' argument);[42] or 'You only die once, and I'd rather go this way than die of lung cancer' (an example of the 'lesser evil' or 'minimax' principle).[43]

However, the main factor in adaptation to danger is probably emotional. The physiological 'wave of anxiety' no longer occurs, or occurs in a modified form. This learning process is gradual, and the initial stages suggest the opposite. The first experience of parachute-jumping, or rock-climbing, may be more frightening than the participant had expected; the fear may then become generalised to other stimuli connected with the dangerous event.[44] The thought of subsequent attempts may thus seem much more frightening than the initial attempt. The anxiety can build up to such an extent that the individual refuses to participate any further. Normal training procedures for learning to dive or climb avoid this problem by increasing the dangers very gradually, so that the novice never experiences a disrupting level of anxiety. Other experiences, like parachute-jumping, are all-or-none affairs, and relatively little can be done to reduce the initial shock. However, those parachutists who are willing to repeat the experience do gradually gain control of their fear. Epstein and Fenz[45] found that novices reported maximum anxiety just before the jump, while experienced parachutists were most anxious some time before the jump and were relatively calm at the time of the jump. Baddeley[46] suggests that the same is true of divers. Experienced participants learn to displace their anxieties away from the critical period by 'rehearsing' them beforehand at a less dangerous moment.

Many types of adaptation have been discussed in this book –

physiological, perceptual, intellectual and emotional. They all contribute to man's ability to survive comfortably and perform efficiently in a wide range of different environments.

NOTES

1 'Scottish Mountaineering Accidents, 1970–71', *Scottish Mountaineering Club Journal*, 1972, Vol. 30, pp. 90–1.

2 G. A. Miller, 'The magical number seven, plus or minus two', *Psychol. Rev.*, 1956, Vol. 63, pp. 81–97.

3 Tom Patey gives an amusing account of a new route which he graded as Difficult, which appeared to be approximately the same route as another party had graded Very Severe. '. . . The original Very Severe line was christened *Oh!* The 1968 Difficult line is therefore entitled *Oh Dear!* It did seem to be the natural line as well as the longest, so both routes must be within striking distance of each other (although presumably not identical?)', *Scottish Mountaineering Club Journal*, 1970, Vol. 29, p. 320.

4 H. McInnes, *Scottish Climbs* (Vols 1 and 2), London: Constable, 1971.

5 The Alpine system includes pluses and minuses, to indicate subgrades of the numerical grades. Only those climbs have been selected where a similar degree of subgrading could be deduced from the Scottish Mountaineering Club District Guides. The selection and subgrading was done by Dr. Peter Murray-Rust and Mr. John Evans of the University of Stirling.

6 *Triton*, June 1972, p. 121.

7 R. W. Kates, 'The perception of storm hazard on the shores of Megalopolis', Ch. 4 in *Environmental Perception and Behavior*, edited by D. Lowenthal, University of Chicago, Department of Geography, Research Paper No. 109, Chicago, 1967.

8 T. F. Saarinen, 'Perception of the drought hazard on the Great Plains', University of Chicago, Department of Geography, Research Paper No. 106, Chicago, 1966.

9 T. F. Saarinen, 'Attitudes towards weather modification: A study of Great Plains farmers', in *Human Dimensions of Weather Modification*, edited by W. R. D. Sewell, University of Chicago, Department of Geography, Research Paper No. 105, Chicago, 1966.

10 J. Sonnenfeld, 'Environmental perception and adaptation level in the Arctic', Ch. 3 in *Environmental Perception and Behavior*, edited by D. Lowenthal, University of Chicago, Department of Geography, Research Paper No. 109, Chicago, 1967.

11 P. R. Gould and R. R. White, 'The mental maps of British school leavers', *Regional Studies*, 1968, Vol. 2, pp. 161–82.

12 H. H. Kelley, 'Attribution theory in social psychology'. In *Nebraska Symposium on Motivation*, Vol. 15, edited by D. Levine, Lincoln: University of Nebraska Press, 1967, pp. 192–238.

13   E. Walster, 'Assignment of responsibility for an accident', *J. Personality and Social Psychology*, 1966, Vol. 3, pp. 73–9.

14   J. Cohen, *Behaviour in Uncertainty*, New York: Basic Books, 1964.

15   W. Bonatti, *On the Heights* (translated by L. F. Edwards), London: Rupert Hart-Davis, 1964.

16   M. J. Lerner and C. H. Simmons, 'Observer's reaction to the "innocent victim": compassion or rejection?', *J. Personality and Social Psychology*, 1966, Vol. 4, pp. 203–10.

17   *The Guardian*, 3 June 1970.

18   C. Bonington, 'Eigerwand', p. 48 in *The Book of Modern Mountaineering*, edited by M. Milne, London: Arthur Baker Ltd, 1968.

19   *Scottish Mountaineering Club Journal*, 1970, Vol. 29, p. 328.

20   *The Observer*, 27 February 1972, p. 11.

21   B. N. Farr, 'Seat belts – the proportion of cars fitted and of occupants using them', Road Research Laboratory, Crowthorne, Berkshire, Report LR 342, 1970.

22   H. Drasdo, 'Education and the Mountain Centres', Tyddyn Gabriel, Melin-y-Coed, Llanwrst, Denbighshire: H. Drasdo, 1972.

23   N. Kogan and M. A. Wallach, 'Risk-taking as a function of the situation, the person and the group', in *New Directions in Psychology III*, foreword by T. M. Newcomb, New York: Holt, Rinehart & Winston, 1967.

24   I. D. Brown, 'Safer drivers', *Brit. J. Hosp. Med.*, October 1970, pp. 441–50.

25   J. Cohen and M. Hansel, *Risk and Gambling*, London: Longmans, Green & Company, 1956.

26   F. J. Kelly and D. J. Baer, 'Physical challenge as a treatment for delinquency', *Crime and Delinquency*, October 1971, pp. 437–45.

27   *The Guardian*, 29 November 1971.

28   T. Patey, 'Apes or ballerinas?', *Mountain*, May 1969 (Reprinted in: T. Patey, *One Man's Mountains*, London: Gollancz, 1971, pp. 212–15).

29   J. R. L. Anderson, *The Ulysses Factor*, London: Hodder & Stoughton, 1970.

30   C. W. Valentine, *The Experimental Psychology of Beauty*, London: Methuen, 1962.

31   K. H. Craik, 'Environmental psychology', in *New Directions in Psychology IV*, foreword by T. M. Newcomb, New York: Holt, Rinehart & Winston, 1970.

32   F. W. Warburton and J. E. Kane, 'Personality related to sport and physical ability', Ch. 4 in *Readings in Physical Education*, edited by J. E. Kane, London: Physical Education Association, 1966.

33   A. K. Nichols, 'The personality of divers (and other sportsmen)', *Underwater Association Report*, 1969, pp. 62–6.

34   D. C. Kendrick, 'The relationship of mental tolerance to emotional and intellectual behaviour before, during, and after physical activity', *The Encyclopedia of Sports Sciences and Medicine*, edited by H. S. Hyman, New York: Collier-MacMillan, 1971.

35   H. E. Ross, 'Personality of student divers', *Underwater Association Report*, 1968, pp. 59–62.

36   M. Zuckerman and N. Cohen, 'Sources of reports of visual and

auditory sensations in perceptual-isolation experiments', *Psychol. Bull.*, 1964, Vol. 62, pp. 1–20.
37   J. Slocum, *Sailing Alone Around the World*, London: Rupert Hart-Davis, 1948.
38   N. Tomalin and R. Hall, *The Strange Voyage of Donald Crowhurst*, London: Hodder & Stoughton, 1970.
39   'Oxford University Expedition to Iceland, 1947', *Bull. Oxford Univ. Exploration Club*, Vol. 1, 1948.
40   J. C. Lilly, 'Mental effects of reduction of ordinary levels of physical stimuli on intact, healthy persons', *Psychiatric Research Reports*, 1956, Vol. 5, pp. 1–9.
41   D. I. Warren, 'Status inconsistency theory and flying saucer sightings', *Science*, 1970, Vol. 170, pp. 599–603.
42   For a discussion of 'lesser peril', and other solutions to problems of 'Cognitive dissonance', see R. Brown, 'Models of attitude change', in *New Directions in Psychology, Vol. 1*; foreword by T. M. Newcomb, New York: Holt, Rinehart & Winston, 1962.
43   For a discussion of the 'minimax principle', and other decision rules, see W. Edwards, 'The theory of decision-making', *Psychol. Bull.*, 1954, Vol. 51, pp. 380–417.
44   For a discussion of emotional conditioning, and other reactions to stress, see I. L. Janis, *Stress and Frustration*, New York: Harcourt Brace Jovanovich, 1971.
45   S. Epstein and W. D. Fenz, 'Steepness of approach and avoidance gradients in humans as a function of experience: theory and experiment', *J. exp. Psychol.*, 1965, Vol. 70, pp. 1–12.
46   A. D. Baddeley, 'Selective attention and performance in dangerous environments', *Brit. J. Psychol.*, 1972, Vol. 63, pp. 537–46.

Index